THE FIRST GENTLEMAN

The Role of the Female Pastor's Husband

DR. JACQUELINE TUGGLE TAYLOR

WESTBOW
PRESS
A DIVISION OF THOMAS NELSON

Cover designed by Mr. Aulander Skinner, III
Reflections Digital Media a subsidiary of Reflections Technologies
website: www.reflectiontechs.com
email: reflectiontechs@gmail.com

WestBow Press books may be ordered through booksellers or by contacting:

WestBow Press
A Division of Thomas Nelson
1663 Liberty Drive
Bloomington, IN 47403
www.westbowpress.com
1-(866) 928-1240

ISBN: 978-1-4497-3665-1 (hc)
ISBN: 978-1-4497-3664-4 (sc)
ISBN: 978-1-4497-3663-7 (e)

Library of Congress Control Number: 2012901116

Scripture taken from the King James Version of the Bible, unless otherwise cited.

Printed in the United States of America

WestBow Press rev. date: 5/8/2012

To my husband, Jarris,
who is "the wind beneath my wings."

CONTENTS

LIST OF TABLES

FOREWORD

Nine of the ten true heroes of this book awoke one day to find out that the person they married now had received a call to ministry and were determined to answer it. That would have been a steep enough mountain to climb. They would have to learn to live with the constant clash of covenants, the blurring of lines between private moments and public faces, the relentless intrusion into home life of this corporate other called the community of faith, and their consignment to the shadows or at least to second violin when the spotlight was turned on the stage.

Mountain enough, but there was more; for in this story the pastor was a woman and the pastor's spouse was a man. That meant there would also be clashes with assigned gender roles, roles that ran deep in the prevailing culture. There would be occasional if not constant clashes with cherished assumptions about power, hierarchy, and protocol. A case in point: how do you as husband respond when the leadership of the pastor (your wife) is publically criticized by someone in the church?

I am so grateful that Jacqueline Taylor did not settle for the resigned separation of the church leader's public service and private life that I see many clergy settling for these days. The way many clergy families seem to deal with the mountain of conflicting covenants is to ignore that it exists by drawing a rigid line between the personal life and public commitment. The pastor lives parallel lives; the pastor's spouse disavows connection, sometimes even basic sympathy for his or her spouses call. But this goes against the grain of the church's own wisdom from Martin Luther's parsonage to the tradition in

Black, Hispanic, and Korean churches of First Lady, and now, at least in the House of God Church and the other congregations surveyed in this project, First Gentleman.

Step by step the husband of the woman pastor, while establishing their own identity and worth, must grow into the unique call to support their spouse's ministry. Through the pondering of biblical couples such as of Deborah and Lapidoth, Priscilla and Aquila; through the mining the story of the emerging equalitarian leadership of the House of God Church; and most of all, through a careful ethnographic study of ten First Gentlemen, Jacqueline Taylor outlines some of those steps. And in doing that she makes a significant contribution to the life of the church in the twenty-first century.

Dr. Lewis A. Parks
Professor of Theology, Ministry, and Congregational
Development and Director of the Doctor of
Ministry Program
Wesley Theological Seminary
Washington, DC

ACKNOWLEDGMENTS

I acknowledge foremost, that God the Father and His Son, Jesus Christ, and the Holy Ghost is the center of my life. With blessing, glory, wisdom, thanksgiving, honor, power, and might, I thank God for my inheritance as His child. Let me also acknowledge my family members, the "inner circle": my husband, Jarris Sr., who has never doubted my vision; my son, Dr. Jarris Jr. and my sister, Dr. Melva Tuggle Owens, whose expertise in research answered the "how and why" questions for me. My daughters, their spouses, and my grandchildren have served as my "encouragement corner": Maria Taylor; Monica and Christopher Coffee; Patrice Taylor; Collette and Abiodun Adamolekun; Dionne, Natasha, Dominik, Amira, and Jordan Taylor; Monae, Deannè, and Nicole Herrington; Ava Coffee; and Corey Adamolekun. My prayer warriors who continuously kept my name before the Lord included my brother and sister-in-law, Reverend Dr. Melvin B. Tuggle II and "First Lady" Brenda Tuggle; sisters-in-law, Jean Bradley and Diane Moye; and uncle Carl Redd. I also appreciated the vigilance of Aunt Mary Redd and Cousin Carla Williams, who would keep me awake in the early mornings or late nights while I keyed into the computer. Indeed, all of the above are my armor bearers.

I am grateful for much love and support from my surrogate sons Jesse Tetterton, Desmond Smith, and Brian Williams, who acknowledge the "ties that bind." Special thanks to the insight of cousins Keaira Still and Karon Moore, and my niece, Twilla Taylor, in assisting me in editing and proofreading. Special accolades for the perseverance of Twilla and Karon for going the last mile of the way with me, during the final hours of "tying up loose ends." To my father, the late Melvin B. Tuggle, I, and especially my mother, a praying, God-fearing woman, the late Gladys M. Tuggle who believed in the proverb, "that God will make a way out of no way." My two special aunts, the late Elizabeth Moore and the late Grace Conigland who provided temporal relief to my family when I was a child. Thank you to the remaining of my extended family members for their love and support. In concluding recognition of my family members, I must acknowledge that my journey at Wesley Theological Seminary was inspired by my brother-in-law, the late Reverend Jerome Lamont Owens.

My encounters with individuals outside of the family unit and whose lives have greatly influenced me are appreciated. Thank God for my church family, who constantly cover me with their prayers. Much love to Dr. Rebecca W. Fletcher, chief overseer and senior bishop of the House of God Church Keith Dominion, and State Elder Kenneth Ellis, prelate of the House of God Churches in the District of Columbia, Maryland, Virginia, and California for sharing their spiritual insight and guidance. Chief Helpers Dillard, Allen and Lott and their spouses, Deaconess Tamara Ellis, Dr. Martha J. Thomas, Dr. and Mrs. Clary K. Butler, Sr., Dr. and Mrs. Semmie Z. Taylor, Sr., State Elder Minnie Crawford, State Elder Olivia Wallace, Dr. and Mrs. Andrew Williams, Reverend Neta Walker, (Essex HOGC Assistant Pastor), Elder Linda Carter and Exhorter Beverly Tripline (Pastor's Helpers), Dr. Emanuel Williams, Deacon Michael Randolph, Deaconess Barbara Elliott, Deaconess Katie Jackson, and all of my Essex and Universal Church family: co-laborers who can get a prayer through. To Apostle Patricia Jones, a new found friend in the Lord. I welcome her spiritual insight. To the late Rev. Dr. Edward M. Revels, my first Pastor, at Saint Paul Community Baptist Church, who knew and believed God called women into ministry. He took me under his tutelage and blessed me with a scholarship to the Maryland Baptist School of Religion where I eventually matriculated in the theology track. Nevertheless, let me forever maintain a special love in my heart for Elder Ruth Brown whose perseverance and persistence in articulating to me the Word of God "in a more perfect way." For this cause I was led to embrace the teachings of the House of God; and to accept as my spiritual covering this Church best for my soul salvation journey.

My pastoral counseling journey at Wesley Theological Seminary has allowed me to interact with a cadre of professional educators, all of whom I cannot name at this writing. However, those who left a thumbprint on my heart and mind include the following: Dr. Lewis A. Parks, Professor of Theology, Ministry, and Congregational Development and Director of the Doctor of Ministry Program, for his encouragement and spirituality which served as a beacon that guided me as I matriculated; Dr. Mary Clark Moschella's eloquent presentation of ethnography, which inspired me to further study this science that is relevant for all pastoral counselors to pursue; Dr. Valerie Leyva, assistant professor of social work at California State University (Stanislaus) and adjunct professor at Wesley: "a social worker extraordinaire" whose sensitivity to the vocation of ministers and their need for expertise in counseling individuals and families persuaded me to recommend her as my reader for the initial project paper on this topic. It was the counseling techniques she taught that inspired me to use the methodology employed in this study; Dr. Beverly Mitchell, who consistently extracts the best gifts a student possesses while striving for mastery, is a blessing; Mrs. Rebecca Scheirer, program administrator of the doctor of ministry programs, who is the students' best friend for resources available in the program and a special "godsend"; and to my colleagues of the 2011 graduating class of practical theology for pastors, chaplains, and clinicians track at Wesley, who demonstrated that love and respect still exist for the matriarchs of our culture. Thanks to all I have encountered on my journey, and especially to God for His manifold blessings in which He "daily loadeth" me with benefits (Psalm 68:19).

INTRODUCTION

This theological research project has been conducted as an ethnographic study as presented by Mary Clark Moschella in her book, *Ethnography as a Pastoral Practice: An Introduction.* Ethnography is about the relationship of listening to, observing, being with, and interpreting a community.[1] Dr. Moschella's book shows that we, as pastors, are more effective as compassionate and understanding caregivers if we hear individuals "in their cultural complexity."[2] It is through hearing individuals' narratives that a pastor learns the otherness of a culture and in so doing is able to co-author[3] and reshape his or her thinking. For this reason, an ethnographic study of the role of a female pastor's husband will be used to clarify questions that may arise in religious practice and provide a guide for further research; perhaps it will foster change or transformation for future generations.

In this ethnography, I will study the husbands of female pastors at the church I attend, the House of God which is the Church of the Living God, the Pillar and Ground of the Truth Without Controversy, Inc. Keith Dominion, I Timothy 3:15-16 (House of God Church or HOGC). The House of God Church is a Pentecostal Holiness church that teaches the doctrine of Jesus Christ. It is a Bible-based church that believes the Holy Ghost/Holy Spirit dwells in believers and is evidenced by them primarily speaking in other and unknown tongues as the Spirit of God gives utterance (Acts 2:1-4).

---

[1] Mary Clark Moschella, *Ethnography as a Pastoral Practice: An Introduction.* (Cleveland: Pilgrim Press, 2008), viii.

[2] Moschella, XV.

[3] Moschella, 237.

The church also believes that possessing the Holy Spirit empowers the believer to live an exemplary life.

Observations in the church community reveal, traditionally, that the role of the first spouse of the church has revolved around the role of the pastor's wife (the first lady). This project will focus on the role of the husband or "first gentleman" in the church of the female pastor. Presently, there are no guidelines for the role of female pastors' husbands. The question to be researched is, "What is the role of the female pastor's husband in the House of God Church, Pentecostal Holiness denomination?"

Overview

This ethnographic study consists of four chapters and a conclusion. Chapter 1 addresses the theological debate concerning women in leadership positions and includes discussion of the purpose of the study, assumptions concerning husbands and wives and pastors and their spouses, and finally, a presentation of the overarching project research questions guiding the project.

Chapter 2 is a review of literature and contains two sections. Part I presents theological implications of women in leadership positions and the role of their spouses. Part I contains discussion of sexism in religion, Egyptian and Hellenistic influences on the role of women in leadership, assumptions of pre-modern and contemporary scholars concerning women as religious leaders, post-modern interpretations of women's roles in the church (the African American and East Asian experiences), the role of pastors and their spouses, the role of pastors and their spouses from a male perspective, the role of pastors and their spouses from a female perspective, and lastly, a comparison of male and female pastors. Part II is a theological analysis of leadership and ministry roles of women. Biblical case studies of Deborah and Lapidoth (Barak), Hulduh and Shallum, Mary and Joseph, and Priscilla and Aquila are analyzed.

Chapter 3 describes the ethnographic tools and methodology used to complete the study. It is separated into three sections. Part I contains the methodology: a description and purpose of the brief counseling strategies theory used to conduct the research, an explanation of the brief counseling strategies theory, an instrumentation and formulation of the survey and interview questions, and a description of how the survey and interview questions were linked to the research. Part II includes a description of how the project was implemented, counseling prerequisites, and plans for how the study was ethically accountable. Part III provides a historical background of the House of God Church founder and co-laborers, a description of the modern day House of God Church, and a description of male and female pastors and their spouses within the House of God Church.

Chapter 4 is a presentation and analysis of project results. It contains survey and interview results, analysis of findings, and reflections on respondents' recommendations.

The conclusion contains reflexivity of the study and reflection of findings, a discussion of future uses and implications of project findings, and recommendations with next steps for future study.

CHAPTER 1

THEOLOGICAL DEBATE
CONCERNING WOMEN
IN LEADERSHIP POSITIONS

As a married female leader in my church, I am aware that for many years, there has been a desire to have written guidelines for the role of the female pastor's husband. Traditionally, in the House of God Church, the wife of a male pastor has always been recognized as the "first lady." The husbands of female pastors are recognized as supporters of their wives but are never addressed as the "first gentleman."

The House of God Church Keith Dominion was established in 1903 by an African American Methodist named Mary Lena Lewis Tate (1871-1930).[4] The Wesleyan Methodist movement in North America during the nineteenth century opened the door for women such as Bishop Tate to preach and serve as leaders in the church.[5] Bishop Tate established the church on the premise that there is equality for all. Male and female alike are appointed to hold official positions such as deacons, pastors, elders, and bishops if qualified in the House of God Church, a policy dating from 1908.[6] This

---

[4]   *The Constitution Government and Decree of the Church of the Living God, the Pillar and Ground of the Truth.* Nashville, TN: The New and Living Way Publishing Co., 1989 Reprint. 4.

[5]   Melvin Dieter, *Great Holiness Classics: Volume Four The Nineteenth-Century Holiness Movement.* Kansas City, Missouri: Beacon Hill Press of Kansas City, 1998, 31-32.

[6]   *Constitution Government,* 6-7

doctrinal belief is supported by the Holy Scriptures: "There is neither Jew nor Greek, there is neither bond nor free, there is neither male nor female: for ye are all one in Christ Jesus" (Galatians 3:28, KJV). It is also addressed in the Constitution of the House of God Church, which denounces segregation, discrimination, and prejudices among the membership.[7]

Purpose of Study

The purpose of this study is to conduct qualitative research and demonstrate that the role of the female pastor's husband is equally as important as the role of the male pastor's wife in the House of God Church Keith Dominion. This study is intended to benefit the husbands by enlivening them through "weaving human and divine stories"[8] and proving there is a definitive role for them to portray.

The Theological Debate

Female leadership has been a topic of debate for centuries between theologians and laity, Christians and non-Christians, as well as men and women. This study will present a theological analysis of the debate concerning male and female roles in leadership positions and ministry. An analysis of the role of the female pastor's spouse, the effects of sexism in religion, and how it has influenced the ecclesiology of the church will be examined as well. Reflections of case studies employing biblical narratives of couples in the Bible will be used to substantiate the roles of women leaders and their spouses. Each scenario identifies the particular role of the husband and the wife, specifically when the wife is the spiritual leader. The narratives portrayed are Joshua's account of Lapidoth, the husband of Deborah, in Judges 4:4; the account of Shallum, the husband of

---

[7]   *Constitution Government,* 58.

[8]   Herbert Anderson and Edward Foley, *Mighty Stories, Dangerous Rituals: Weaving Together the Human and the Divine.* San Francisco: Jossey-Bass, 1998, xiii.

Huldah, in 2 Kings 22:14 and 2 Chronicles 34:22; the account of Joseph, the husband of Mary, in Matthew 1 and Luke 3; and the apostle Paul's account of Aquila, the husband of Priscilla, in Acts 16:3-5. A comparative analysis of various theologians' interpretations of women called by God to leadership positions in ministry will be discussed.

The House of God Church has been chosen as the target population due to the fact that my husband is the spouse of a female pastor. As I reflect on our years together, it is apparent that God was preparing Deacon Taylor at a young age to be "one flesh" with me long before we met. This is evidenced by the support that I receive from him in church and at home. Not only was he prepared to be my "help meet," but God prepared him to be the spouse of a spiritual leader who has authority over him in the church. This study focuses on the vital role of that "first man" or "first gentleman" in the House of God Church. It does us well to be reminded that the closest person to the female pastor, besides God, is her husband.

Assumptions Concerning Husbands and Wives/Pastors and Spouses Relationships

For centuries, the roles of the relationship between pastor and spouse and husband and wife for many has been based on the assumption that only the male can be a pastor or spiritual leader over people. Great debates between theologians are unending on this topic. The roles of the husband and wife are viewed naturally and biblically. In times past, the expected role of the wife was to be homemaker, child bearer, child-rearer, nurturer, disciplinarian, and an exemplary wife (Sarah, Rachel, and Hannah are examples). The husband was recognized as the head of the household, breadwinner, protector, and the exemplary husband (Abraham, Lot, and Jacob are examples). In the Old Testament, the husband was the priest of the household (i.e. Noah, Genesis 8:20, and Abram, Genesis 13:18), although the Scriptures acknowledge women prophetesses (preachers) such as Miriam, Deborah, Huldah, and others as having been used by God. In the New Testament, according to 1 Peter

1:9-10, male believers are priests and female believers are priestesses of the priesthood.

> But ye are a chosen generation, a royal priesthood, an holy nation, a peculiar people; that ye should show forth the praises of him who hath called you out of darkness into his marvelous light: Which in time past were not a people, but are now the people of God: which had not obtained mercy, but now have obtained mercy.

According to societal expectations in this modernistic age, husbands and wives are to be supportive to each other in caring for the home and family. Both are apt to exchange roles; in fact, some men are classified as "house husbands." These men care for their children and homes while the wives work. Some women are classified as "career professionals," such as CEOs of Fortune 500 conglomerates. To name just a few professions, others are telephone line repair persons, welders, firefighters, and law enforcement officers. Since the twentieth century, there have been role reversals among males and females in the religious arena. Historically, in the religious community, the pastor of the church was a male, but today, more and more female pastors are leading congregations. In spite of the changes in other professions and vocations, the female pastor continues to perform homemaking duties as well as carry out her ministerial responsibilities.

Overarching Project Research Inquiry Questions

The focus of this study is to examine, from a male perspective, the role of the female pastor's husband. The data collected will be analyzed, and the findings will be presented to a group of clergy and laity in a seminar titled "The Role of the Female Pastor's Husband." The understanding of the participants will be assessed through discussion in a question-and-answer session at the conclusion of the seminar. Input from attendees will be encouraged and used in the development of guidelines for the role of the female pastor's husband.

The presentation of empirical data will support the hypothesis that women are called by God for leadership positions in God's plan of salvation and kingdom building. This suggests that there is a place for husbands of women in leadership positions. The evaluation of biblical roles of husbands and wives in the natural walk of life and spiritual realm will aid in identifying the roles of female pastors and their spouses.

The following research ancillary questions are presented for inquiry:

1. Is God sexist?
2. Does the Bible support women holding leadership positions in a patriarchal society?
3. Does the Bible define a role for the husbands of these female leaders?

I am compelled to seek answers to these questions in an effort to determine the epistemological foundation[9] of the pastor's husband serving in the church and, in addition, to determine if this causal/ predictive puzzle[10] will confirm whether an "unspoken role" already exists for the pastor's husband. Once it has been established that God does call women to leadership positions in ministry, the husbands' responses will support the research thesis statement for this study, "The Role of the Female Pastor's Husband in the House of God Church, Pentecostal Holiness denomination." In concluding this research project, the formation of written guidelines will serve as a reminder to the men and empower them to be transformed into effective "first gentlemen."

---

[9] Mary Field Belenky, Lynne A. Bond, and Jacqueline S. Weinstock, *A Tradition That Has No Name.* New York: Basic Books, 1997, 55.
[10] Moschella, 77.

CHAPTER 2

REVIEW OF LITERATURE

Part I: Theological Implications of Women in Leadership Positions and the Role of Their Spouses

This chapter is interwoven with discussion on the theological debate as to whether women should be pastors or bishops. The infiltration of sexist ideology is the cause of debate as to whether women should lead, in my opinion. It is centered on the interpretations of contemporary theologians of the writings of the apostle Paul concerning the roles of men and women in the church. Empirical data presented will support the hypothesis that women are called by God for leadership positions in the building of His kingdom. A need for a defined role for their husbands will be established in this book. The three ancillary questions being discussed in this chapter are the following: Is God sexist? Does the Bible support women holding leadership positions in a patriarchal society? Does the Bible define a role for the husbands of these female leaders? The first two questions will be addressed here in chapter 2, part I; the final question will be discussed in chapter 2, part II.

Sexism in Religion

Sexism has existed from the start of the first patriarchy; the Greek meaning of patriarch is "father and rule."[11] Joseph Martos and

---

[11]   Joseph Martos and Pierre Hégy, eds., *Equal at the Creation: Sexism, Society, and Christian Thought.* Toronto: University of Toronto Press, 1998, 3.

Pierre Hegy propose that "every human culture has treated men and women differently whether that culture be tribal, nomadic, sedentary, agricultural, industrial, or postindustrial. Differential treatment of men and women according to their sex appears to be endemic to the human condition."[12] Joan Morris writes, "Pliny the Elder tells in his book *Natural History* that information was intentionally hidden regarding the work of women doctors. The opinion of that day was women should be quiet and inconspicuous as possible so that after they are dead no one would know that they had lived."[13]

Sexism is not only found in the secular arena; it is also found in religion. In religion, sexism is found in the debate over woman in ministry. There are some theologians who believe that women are subservient to men, and they use Genesis 3:16b to justify their belief: " . . . and thy desire shall be to thy husband, and he shall rule over thee" (KJV). However, there is no indication from this Scripture that God is saying that woman should desire that all men rule over her, just her husband. The belief in inequality between husband and wife is contrary to Scripture found in Genesis 2:18. God made Eve as a "helpmeet" to Adam. The Hebrew translation of "helpmeet" *(neged)* means a counterpart, mate, or opposite part.[14] Author Bruce Robinson defines "helpmeet" by using the word *ayzer,* meaning co-worker of equal status to Adam, helper, or partner.[15] Therefore, Adam and Eve, as husband and wife, were co-workers of equal status.

---

[12] Martos and Hégy, 3.

[13] Joan Morris, *The Lady Was a Bishop: The Hidden History of Women with Clerical Ordination and the Jurisdiction of Bishops.* New York, New York: The Macmillan Co, 1973, xi.

[14] Spiros Zodhiates, ed., "Hebrew and Chaldee Dictionary" in *The Hebrew-Greek Key Study Bible.* Chattanooga, TN: AMG Publishers, Revised Edition 1991, 76.

[15] Bruce A. Robinson, "Women as Religious Leaders in the Bible and Early Christian Writings." *Ontario Consultants on Religious Tolerance* http://www.religioustolerance.org/femclrg.htm updated September 26, 2008. [accessed July 1, 2010], 1.

Egyptian and Hellenistic Influences on the Role of Women in Leadership

On one occasion, while sitting in my allergist's office, I noticed the front cover of a *National Geographic* magazine. Its caption read, "The She-King of Egypt."[16] It addressed the rule of Hatshepsut, a female who reigned in Egypt for twenty-one years as a man. "What would make a woman of royal descent take on the role of a man and serve as King of Egypt and not Queen of Egypt?" I wondered. Egyptians during the period (fifteenth century BC), were patriarchal and believed that the kingship should pass down from father to son.[17] There was no gender equality among their leaders; men only were to take the headship of the country.[18] It is believed that Hatshepsut stole the kingship from her stepson, Thutmose III, when her husband-brother, Thutmose II, died. Author of the article Chip Brown says that Hatshepsut's remains were discovered in 1903 by Howard Carter, who found them hidden in the ruins of her temple along with the remains of her nurse.[19] Her statues were later found in a pit in front of her temple. It is as if her twenty-one year reign was deliberately obscured in the annals of history.[20] Brown believes that Hatshepsut's stepson, who was of royal blood, succeeded the throne after her death and hid the reign of Hatshepsut.[21]

John Bristow, author of *What Paul Really Said about Women,* contends that the debate concerning women's rights came from the Hellenic culture. He states that the idea that the apostle Paul was chauvinistic was influenced by the writings of Greek philosopher Aristotle, who considered women to be second-class citizens and inferior

---

16   Chip Brown, "Hatshepsut: Ruled Egypt Twenty-One Years as a Man, 1479-1458 B.C." *National Geographic.* 215 no. 4 (April 2009): 88-111.
17   Brown, 99.
18   Ibid.
19   Brown, 105.
20   Ibid.
21   Brown, 98.

to men.[22] This established a traditional method of viewing Paul's insights as being sexually discriminating from a Greek and pagan perspective rather than a Jewish and Christian perspective.[23] Bristow says as a result, the philosophy of "sexual inequality" was born in the minds of individuals in the Jewish cultures when Christianity began to spread throughout the world. Bristow cautions us to study and understand the Greek language because it has meanings that are very different from the English language. This view is quite contrary to other theologians, since patriarchy exists in the book of Genesis with heads of households, such as Adam, Noah, Abraham, priests, and others.

Bristow contends that Paul tried to change the "Aristotle way of thinking" when he wrote Galatians 3:28 (KJV): "There is neither Jew nor Greek, there is neither bond nor free, there is neither male nor female: for ye are all one in Christ Jesus." Paul's goal was to change the ideology of the relationship of Jewish husbands and wives, which is premised on Adam and Eve's condition after the fall, to the new way of modeling husband and wife relationships based on that of Christ and the church. During medieval times, artists portrayed Christ looking in the distance with his hand outstretched and a woman at His feet gazing at His halo. The idea of the Church kneeling at the feet of Jesus is what some interpreted as the relationship between man and wife.[24] I concur with Bristow that the artist's rendition, indeed, is a misrepresentation of the true relationship between husband and wife, and man and woman.[25] The Scriptures do not indicate gender discrimination in God's plan of salvation. God makes no preference that only males are to spread the Gospel message. According to Acts 2:16-18, God chooses to anoint male and female alike to "plant his word in" so they may promulgate the Gospel of Jesus Christ according to His divine and permissive will.

---

[22] John Temple Bristow, *What Paul Really Said About Women: An Apostle's Liberating Views on Equality in Marriage, Leadership, and Love with Study Questions.* New York: HarpersCollins, 1988, 3.

[23] Bristow, 3.

[24] Bristow, 32.

[25] Ibid.

Assumptions of Pre-Modern and Contemporary Scholars Concerning Women As Religious Leaders

In spite of the rejection of some women being ordained as pastors and bishops, contemporary theologians have studied the Scriptures for truth and have been inspired by the divine guidance of the Holy Spirit to write their interpretation. Paul says, "All Scripture is given by inspiration of God, and is profitable for doctrine, for reproof, for correction, for instruction in righteousness: That the man of God may be perfect, thoroughly furnished unto all good works" (2 Timothy 3:16-17, KJV).

The nineteenth-century Holiness Movement in the United States was predicated on the Wesleyan Movement, which was begun in England by John and Charles Wesley. This new religious culture was a combination of Protestant and Roman Catholic traditions and the Hebrew experiences of the Old Testament, which are all significant in the New Testament which introduces Christianity.[26]

Now in the twenty-first century, we find the debate ongoing, as evidenced in a recent article by John Dart. One would surmise that by divine revelation gained through studying the Scriptures, man's perception of gender inequality should have changed in our time. It is appalling that in the twenty-first century, we are still blatantly confronted with male ministers who are dissident over females being ordained pastors and bishops. John Dart, news editor of *The Christian Century* magazine, in an article titled "Female Pastors' Story Rattles SBC Nerves," states that at the same time the Episcopal Church ordained its first female Presiding Bishop, Katharine Jefferts-Schorie, the Southern Baptist Conference (SBC) banned the sale of the *Gospel Today* magazine at LifeWay bookstores (an affiliate of SBC). The magazine cover featured pictures of five "powerful" women pastors who each shepherd over a thousand congregants in their churches. The women honored were Tamara Bennett of This Is Pentecost Ministries in Sacramento; Claudette Copeland of New Creation Christian Fellowship in San Antonio; Bishop Millicent Hunter of the Baptist

---

[26] Melvin Dieter, 23.

Worship Center in Philadelphia; Kimberly Ray of Church on the Rock in Matteson, Illinois; and Sheryl Brady of the River in Durham, North Carolina.[27] These female pastors are noted as being just as successful in ministry as their male counterparts. This is just another example of the theological debate over gender inequity which exists today.

Köstenberger et al., editors of *Women in the Church,* provide a "for or against" argument on the topic of the ordination of women. Robert Yarbough draws attention to theologians K. Stendahl and the late F. F. Bruce, who supported the ideology of re-visitation of Scriptures when addressing the roles of women in ministry.[28] Yarbrough quotes a portion of Stendahl's essay, which criticized liberal theologians for having a "conscious or unconscious tendency to judge and evaluate texts and ideas from the first century by the anachronistic standards of modern Western values and sentiments."[29] Women who have accepted God's call to ministry are well aware of "unfair treatment" to them by both genders. The increase of women in ministry has led to egalitarianism in some denominations and has affected the ecclesiology of religion. Leadership positions are now shared with males and females alike, although there continue to be many men and women who refuse to accept the paradigm shift in religion in the twenty-first century.

Köstenberger et al. provide what they convey as "a fresh analysis" of 1 Timothy 2:9-15. They find it difficult to believe that Paul supported discrimination against women in religious settings, especially since women served as priestesses and goddesses in the free Greek city-

27   John Dart, "'Female Pastors' Story Rattles SBC Nerves" *Christian Century* 125 no.21 (Oct 21 2008): 16-17. http://newfirstsearch.oclc. org/WebZ/FTFETCH? sessionid=fsapp6-51254-gb2iiz2qfbvlk7:entity pagenum=21:0:rule=100 :fetchtype=fulltext: dbname=ATLA_FT:recno =7:resultset=2:ftformat=PDF:format=BI:isbillable=TRUE:numrecs=1:is directarticle=FALSE:entityemailfullrecno=7:entityemailfullresultset=2: entityemailftfrom=ATLA_FT: [accessed May 24, 2010],16.
28   Andreas J. Köstenberger, Thomas R. Schreiner and H. Scott Baldwins, eds., *Women in the Church: A Fresh Analysis of I Timothy 2:9-15.* Grand Rapids, Michigan: Baker Books, 1995. 179.
29   Köstenberger, 179.

states.[30] The negative connotations of 1 Timothy 2:12 make it difficult for the average person to understand what Paul is actually saying. Views of several theologians are presented in this analysis. One view by Thomas R. Schreiner supports the idea that Paul is saying that women are prohibited from teaching men because man was created first. Schreiner, while appealing to women to recognize the creative order of mankind, further contends that women are not banned from teaching; they are only banned from teaching men. To do otherwise, according to Schreiner, would violate the principle of male leadership.[31]

Contemporary theologians, such as Martos and Hegy, Bristow, and the Kroegers, refute the ideology of Schreiner that women are not to be pastors or bishops and are banned from teaching men. They suggest that Paul was really saying something contrary to what has been interpreted for years in 1 Timothy 2:11-12:

> Let the woman learn in silence with all subjection. But I suffer not a woman to teach, nor to usurp authority over the man, but to be in silence

Modern scholars and laity have begun to rethink what Paul is actually saying. Richard and Catherine Kroeger, authors of *I Suffer Not a Woman: Rethinking 1 Timothy 2:11-15 in Light of Ancient Evidence,* support the theory, based on hermeneutical references, that there is gender equality in ministry. The Krogers concur with Bristow that early theologians' traditional interpretations of the Bible were misrepresented based on the fact that during Paul's era, women were teaching men and women. Paul alludes to involvement of women in leadership roles, such as Priscilla instructing Apollos, Lois and Eunice instructing and training Timothy, and Phoebe serving as overseer (bishop) and deacon in the church at Cenchrea.[32] The Kroegers refute the ideology that subjection of women to men is due to the fall of Eve. They ask, "If this

---

30   Köestenberger, 33.

31   Köstenberger, 140.

32   Richard Clark Kroeger and Catherine Clark Kroeger, *I Suffer Not a Woman: Rethinking I Timothy 2:11-15 in Light of Ancient Evidence.* Grand Rapids, Michigan: Baker Book House, 1992, 17.

is true, what can we say about God's redemptive grace?" The authors challenge our thinking when they ask the question, "Are men not held accountable for the sins of their forebears, while women must pay for the sin of their original ancestress?"[33] The answer is emphatically, "No!" God is a God of second chances. He forgives and loves all with an everlasting love, and His mercy endures forever.

The authors admit that the problem with women not being recognized as leaders (pastors and bishops) is a practical as well as a theological problem that must be addressed now and made clear. The Kroegers state that the practical problem with women called into ministry is that some men have said to them, "God did not do so."[34] This is interpreted to say that men are telling women that God did not call them into the ministry. There is also the issue of women being saved in the process of childbearing.[35] The theological problem is concerned with individuals who believe salvation is gained by faith alone. The Kroegers cannot understand how a woman can be saved by childbearing.[36] Today, salvation has come to everyone's "house" that is the temple in which the Holy Ghost dwells. Salvation is for whosoever believeth continuously, whether or not they have given birth to a child, according to John 3:16.

Kroeger and Kroeger's interpretation of 1Timothy 2:11-12 is that a woman teacher or women teachers were teaching congregations contrary doctrine. This statement was not a prohibition of women instructing men.[37] They provide an alternative translation of 1 Timothy 2:11-12: "Let the woman learn in silence with all subjection. But I suffer not a woman to teach, nor to usurp authority over the man, but to be in silence." The interpretation of "learn in silence" and "to usurp authority" means "I do not permit a woman to teach nor to represent herself as originator of man, but she is to be in conformity [with the Scriptures] [or that she keeps it a secret; or learns in peace

---

33 Kroeger, 22.

34 Kroeger, 23-26.

35 Kroeger, 26.

36 Ibid.

37 Kroeger, 81.

or harmony]. For Adam was created first, then Eve."[38] The Kroegers
conclude by saying that Paul was not forbidding women to teach the
Scriptures in 1 Timothy 2:13-14 ("For Adam was first formed, then
Eve. And Adam was not deceived, but the woman being deceived was
in the transgression"), but rather alluding to Timothy refuting heresy
being spread in the church.[39] John Bristow interprets the role of the
female in a leadership position in a different hermeneutical light than
the Kroegers.

Some of the debate concerning women in leadership is based
on the premise that wives are not to usurp authority over their
husbands. The mindset of some chauvinistic men is that wives are to
be totally submissive to them because they make all of the decisions
in the marriage. John Bristow presents new revelation in Ephesians
5:21-23: "Submitting yourselves one to another in the fear of God.
Wives, submit yourselves unto your own husbands, as unto the Lord.
For the husband is *the head* of the wife, even as Christ is the head of
the church: and he is the saviour of the body" (italics mine). Bristow
interprets *head* being the base of the Greek word which Paul used,
kephale (kef-ah-LAY), which means "foremost" as in being a leader,
as opposed to a captain, general, or director: it was not intended to
denote physical head, boss, chief, or ruler.[40]

Ephesians 5:24-25 reads, "Therefore as the church is *subject* unto
Christ, so let the wives be to their own husbands in every thing.
Husbands, *love* your wives, even as Christ also loved the church, and
gave himself for it" (italics mine). Bristow also explains the difference
in English and Greek translation in the phrase *be subject to.* This does
not mean that wives are to be subject to their husbands as a subject is
to his ruler. Instead, Paul uses the Greek word *hupotassomai* (hoop-
o-TASS-o-my) in the active middle voice, according to the Greek
language. The term is to be interpreted to mean that wives in the
marital relationship "give allegiance to," "tend to the needs of," "be
supportive of," "be responsive to," or as in the German translation,

---

38   Kroeger, 103.
39   Kroeger, 117.
40   Bristow, 36-37.

"to place oneself at the disposition of," their husbands.[41] Finally, Bristow defines *love* in this passage with the Greek word *agapao* (ah-ga-PAH-o), which centers around attitudes and actions which involve giving up one's self-interest to serve and care for another's.[42] I perceive this kind of love as being "godly," unconditional, and limitless because it is the love of God, which has descended from the Holy Spirit to indwell in all Christians. We see continuity in God's grace and mercy as He uses whomever He will in ministry.

Other theologians, such as Bruce Robinson, acknowledge that there were women religious leaders in the Bible and in early Christian writings.[43] Robinson indicates that mostly during biblical times, a woman was considered to be chattel or property belonging to her father before she was married and to her husband once she was married. Nevertheless, God openly exalted a few women to positions of leadership with power and authority. Such women included Eve, Miriam, Deborah, Huldah, Anna, Mary the Mother of Jesus, Tabitha, Phillip's four evangelistic daughters, Euodia, Syntche, Phoebe, Junia, and Priscilla.[44] Many of these women became lost in the Scriptures because readers do not know their marital status or anything concerning their backgrounds.

Charles Johnson, in his article "A Word About God's Women," contends, "Women are submitting themselves to the call of God on their lives".[45] He acknowledges without reservations that the Holy Spirit is the one calling women and that they are responding to

---

[41]   Bristow, 37-41.

[42]   Bristow, 41-42.

[43]   Bruce A. Robinson, "Women as Religious Leaders in the Bible and Early Christian Writings." *Ontario Consultants on Religious Tolerance* http://www.religioustolerance.org/femclrg.htm updated September 26, 2008. [accessed July 1, 2010, 1.

[44]   Robinson, 1.

[45]   Charles F. Johnson. "God's Women." *Review and Expositor* 103 no. 3 (Summer 2006): 491-493. http://newfirstsearch.oclc. org/WebZ/FTFETCH?sessionid=fsapp7-51492-gb2nc1mkjhhshj: entitypagenum=8:0:rule=100: fetchtype=fulltext:dbname=ATLA_FT:re cno=10:resultset=1:ftformat=PDF :format=BI:isbillable=TRUE:numrecs

His call in record numbers to proclaim the gospel of Jesus Christ. Johnson also states that the will of God is that He intentionally plans to fill His pulpits with women, as well as men. In light of this statement, it is an indication that we must prepare mentally for more and more women being proactive in ministry. We can conclude that contemporary theological assumptions are supported by Holy Scriptures that women are called and anointed by God to pastor and/or become bishops in a patriarchal society. This answers question number two. Chapter 2, part II, furthermore, will address the answer to question number three, that of the role of the female pastor's husband.

Post-Modern Interpretations of Women's Role in the Church: The African American and the East Asian Experience

The woman of God whom He has anointed to take a leadership position is indeed a virtuous woman and is more valuable than precious gems. God's will transcends the vain imagination of the wisest of mortal men in any ethnic culture. The debate over women in leadership positions in the church is not limited to any particular ethnic group but is prevalent in both the western and eastern hemispheres. Modern-day thoughts on the role of women theologians have been addressed by women like Delores Williams concerning African American women of Western culture and Eunjoo Mary Kim concerning Korean and Japanese women in Eastern culture.

Delores Williams, author of *Sisters in the Wilderness: The Challenge of Womanist God-Talk,* writes to identify the need for African American women theologians to write their own autobiographies of their faith journeys. She recalls her humble beginnings. Raised in the rural South, Ms. Williams poses questions which help readers to discern the stance of the black female theologian. The questions include, "What has been the character of her faith journey?", "What lessons

=1:isdirectarticle=FALSE:entityemailfullrecno=10:entityemailfullresults et=1:entityemailftfrom=ATLA_FT: [accessed June 30, 2010]

has this journey taught?", and "What kind of faith inspires her to continue writing, rewriting, living, and reliving theology in a highly secular, white-and-black world and paying little or no attention to what theologians are saying?"[46] Williams parallels biblical accounts with the struggle of black women (mothers) in their effort to support their community and maintain a deep-rooted trust in God.

Williams utilizes the phrase *womanist,* meaning the black woman's affirmations of her faith in God, in spite of her personal struggles in providing contributions in supporting the black community.[47] She hopes that her book transforms the church community's sexist view of black women who have resisted and have risen above oppression. According to Williams, it is time for theology to be corrected in view of the woman's role in the patriarchal and androcentric (the woman's role is defined by the male and is evaluated as less socially significant as the traditional male role) biases in African American churches where these women's faith rests in a God who "makes a way out of no way."[48] This belief in God has shaped their theology and exemplifies the struggle of African American women.

Williams contends that presently, the influence of the black female in the African American community has been paramount. Black mothers have demonstrated the ability to embrace religion as their source of emotional, psychological, and spiritual strength in the development of the black community. Williams also notes that the presence of black spiritual hymns created during slavery indicated a positive perspective of the strength of the black mother. Although she was in bondage, the African American mother was able to overcome difficult tasks by depending on God and her religious faith for deliverance.[49] However, this does not negate the tension that was created because of the consciousness and dependence of the black mother in God. We then find the transference of authority

---

[46]   Delores Williams, *Sisters in the Wilderness, The Challenge of Womanist God-Talk.* Maryknoll, New York: Orbis Books, 2004 ninth printing, ix.

[47]   Williams, xiv.

[48]   Williams, xii.

[49]   Williams, 37.

into the hands of the male figure. Once separated from his family and used as a stud on another plantation, the African American male is now placed in the patriarchal model. Due to this historical fact, the institutionalization of various black denominations has placed the black male in authority in the black church community, where women are once again oppressed.[50]

Williams contends it is the nurturing of the black community which recognized Rosa Parks for fighting racism as a catalyst for social change in America. Nevertheless, sexism still exists among male theologians who contend that black mothers maintain their role as nurturers by rejecting ordination for these women in the church.

The black family strove to pattern after the patriarchal model of mainstream society by having black women assumed by their rightful roles in the home.[51] Although sexual exploitation existed, it was decreased by black women who refused to take the role of white females by not engaging in sexual relations with white males. Williams concludes her narrative by saying that males, females of the majority society, and black males' social roles have been a negative influence in demeaning the role of the black woman. This matriarchal model has always been the pillar of strength to the black family and church community, which further indicated the existence of gender and racial inequality in the western hemisphere.

Eunjoo Mary Kim discusses the marginalization of Korean and Japanese women preachers who hold Christ as the center of their lives. Kim states that these women "now live as individuals in their societies who are united to participate in the transforming work of the Holy Spirit based on Acts 1 and 2."[52] These women derive from patriarchal

---

50   Williams, 41.

51   Williams, 72.

52   Eunjoo Mary Kim, "The Holy Spirit and New Marginality." *Journal for Preachers* 25 No. 4 Pentecost (2002): 26-31. http://newfirstsearch. oclc.org/WebZ/FTFETCH?   sessionid=fsapp7-51492-gb2nwhtl- xvxqer:entitypagenum=3:0:rule= 100:fetchtype= fulltext:dbname=ATLA_ FT:recno=1:resultset=1:ftformat=PDF:format=BI:isbillable=TRUE:numre cs=1:isdirectarticle=FALSE:entityemailfullrecno=1:entityemailfullresults et=1:entityemailftfrom=ATLA_FT: [accessed June 30, 2010], 26.

cultures where the men tend to denigrate women by the rules they enforce. The women, through marginalization in the secular world and church, tolerate the domination of this patriarchal system.[53] This confirms that the debate over women with leadership positions in ministry is not limited to one culture, but is a multi-culture debate.

Asian women believe that they have been called by the Holy Spirit who has renewed them and given them new lives in ministry. Although the women are liberated by the Spirit, their ministries are limited to the indigenous, to orphans, to nursing home residents, to those who are incarcerated, and to other areas that have been abandoned by the church under a patriarchal system. Kim acknowledges that the creative work of these women in the ministry is guided by the indwelling of the Holy Spirit, who reconciled and inspired them to carry out the work of the Gospel. Kim declares that "The Gospel of the risen Christ is the Gospel of New Marginality."[54] She quotes author Jung Young Lee's saying, "The Spirit of God comes to their ministerial places where oppression and self-alienation are present and transforms their marginal places into 'a new and creative core' where a new reality emerges. Through the power of the Spirit, they live in the new margin, not as victims of centrality pushed off to the periphery by the dominant masculine group, but as God's partners in a new creative center where the Spirit dwells and acts for the wholeness of God."[55]

The narratives of Williams and Kim recognize that gender inequality in ministry is cross-cultural. Yet, the debate continues; however, it does not negate those who have conceded that women are called by God to leadership positions as pastors and bishops.

The Role of Pastors and Their Spouses

It is obvious that the leadership styles of men will vary in the spiritual realm, as it is in the natural. According to Jim Wright, noted photographer and husband of a female pastor, church officials

---

[53]   Kim, 26.

[54]   Kim, 28.

[55]   Kim, 27.

expect him to be employed outside of the church due to their inability to provide for him and his family. However, Mr. Wright is expected to be active in the church, just as the other members. At the writing of his article, he served as member of the Christian education and property committees and as a Sunday school teacher.[56] According to Mr. Wright, his role is not defined as the pastor's husband, and there is nothing with which to compare his role. He expressed comfort in what he was doing and not having other demands placed upon him.

Another article that specifically addresses the role of the female pastor's husband is by Dr. Lillian Daniel, pastor of First Congregational Church of Glen Ellyn in Glen Ellyn, Illinois.[57] She contends that in order for a pastor to maintain a successful marriage with less pressure, the role of the pastor's spouse must not be ignored. The spouse must recognize her ministry, and she must recognize that her spouse has the option to volunteer for a particular project. The couple must recognize the dynamics of both their careers and not neglect family life. Daniel emphasizes the support each must provide because of the fact that they are engaged in a worship community and that the husband's role is not to be considered an unpaid part-time job.[58] A female pastor's husband must realize that God should always be first in the couple's lives. It is at this point that self-actualization occurs: when "God is within us."[59]

---

[56] Jim Wright, *Notes from a Pastor's Husband.* Christian Ministry 17 no 1 Ja 1986. ISSN: 0033-4138, 12

[57] Lillian Daniel, "The Pastor's Husband: Redefining Expectations." *Christian Century.* 126 no 14 July 14, 2009, p. 28-31. http://newfirstsearch.oclc.org/WebZ/FSQUERY?format=BI:next=html/records. html:bad=html/records.html:numrecs=10:sessionid=fsapp4-56801-gb14apnd-d0hir:entitypagenum=24:0:searchtype=basic [accessed 5/24/10], 29.

[58] Daniel, 30.

[59] Felicity B. Kelcourse, ed., *Human Development and Faith: Life Cycle Stages of Body, Mind, and Soul* (St. Louis, Missouri: Chalice, 2004), 291.

The Role of Pastors and Their Spouses from a Male Perspective

I found it interesting that The African Methodist Episcopal Church (AME) has already become a forerunner in addressing the needs of clergy spouses and their families. In a telephone interview with Mrs. Irene Montegues, second president of the Second Episcopal District Clergy Family Organization, she shared information on a conference held in Baltimore, Maryland, in October 2010. The organization met to discuss and resolve concerns that male and female clergy, their spouses, and their children are confronted with in today's changing times. In their monthly newsletter, Brother Melvin Williams, president of the Baltimore conference, wrote an article about the workshop presented by Reverend Marvin Glenn, husband of Pastor Barbara Glenn of First AME Church in Gaithersburg, Maryland (of the Washington Conference). According to Mrs. Montegues, Reverend Glenn is the oldest male spouse of a female pastor represented in the conference. The title of the workshop was "The Role of the Male Spouse."

Mr. Williams provides us with a list of responsibilities presented by the husbands as to what they consider their role as male spouses[60]:

> The husband is to help his wife in ministry because they are in it together.
> He must remember that women need love and men need respect.
> Husbands must accept the fact that the female pastor has authority in the church and her husband has the authority in the home, although the wife may run the home.
> The husband must remember that his role in the secular world may make it difficult to accept his wife's authority in her role as pastor in the church.
> Because his wife is pastor, the husband must accept her authority in the church.

---

[60] Melvin Williams, Conn-M-SWAW0 Plus PKs Newsletter. *The Role of the Male Spouse*, Baltimore, Maryland Conference,: October 2010, 4.

The male spouse is the eyes and ears for his wife/ preacher/pastor.

The husband must accept the fact that when the wife acknowledges that God is first in her life, he will be hurt because he is no longer first. However, a husband that is grounded in the truth will soon get over the hurt.

The male spouse must learn that there are times when he cannot come to his wife's rescue. There are times when his wife is being hurt or lied to by others. The husband must learn when and where not to intervene. He must restrain himself by not trying to take over when things are not favorable. Avoidance in doing this may prevent embarrassment to the wife. Men should make suggestions when they are alone with their wives; and they should strategize and develop a plan for the husband to signal the wife to alert her when things are not quite right.

The husband should always encourage his wife by praising his wife/pastor/preacher.

The husband should be cautious of what he says because someone is looking and listening to him. The husband should always be friendly to everyone, but realize that not everyone will be his friend.

The Role of Pastors and Their Spouses from a Female Perspective

The late Dr. Weptanomah W. Carter, in her book *The Black Minister's Wife as a Participant in the Redemptive Ministry of Her Husband*, has adequately presented the responsibilities of the pastor's spouse; however, the book is written with the focus on the spouse being a female. Dr. Carter presents the female spouse as being one who serves by the pastor's side, is an understanding mate, is a homemaker, is a leader of Christian ministries, is a guide of church decorum and manners, and is a model to the people.[61] Emphasis is placed on the

---

61 Weptanomah W. Carter, *The Black Minister's Wife: as a Participant in the Redemptive Ministry of Her Husband*. Baltimore, Maryland: Gateway Press, Inc., 1995, 27.

spouse's responsibility to God first, then to the church, and to the home.[62] The redemptive ministry that the spouse should be engaged in is the ministry inclusive of listening, helps, Christian education, evangelism, social services, communications, printed word, and audio communication, in addition to dealing with tensions and precaution in not overshadowing the pastor.[63] The results of this project will hopefully clarify and differentiate the role of the female pastor's husband, just as Dr. Carter has identified the role of the male pastor's spouse.

A Comparison of Male and Female Pastors

Peter Jarvis' research findings categorize three areas of competency for men and women clergy. They are 1) vocation and organization; 2) laity; and 3) colleagueship.[64]

Vocation and organization has traditionally indicated that female ministers are client-oriented (devoted to the needs of the congregants) and the male's role is geared to loyalty to the organization. Overall, male and female ministers agree that ***laity*** should not have overriding power over the ecclesiastical functions of the minister.

Colleagueship: both males and females value co-operation with their colleagues, female ministers more so. The collegial relationships assist one another in maintaining paradigm shifts and provide an assessment of their current abilities.

Edward Morgan's research findings indicated that individuals with both male and female traits are more effective as pastoral leaders. Morgan contends that pastoral masculinity combined organically with pastoral femininity (and vice versa with females) enables the

---

[62]   Carter, 46-58.

[63]   Carter, 69-83.

[64]   Peter Jarvis, "Men and Women Ministers of Religion." *Modern Churchman* 22 no. 4 (1979): 149-158. http://newfirstsearch.oclc.org/ WebZ/FSQUERY?   format=BI:next=html/records.html:bad=html/ records.html:numrecs=10:sessionid =fsapp4-56801-gb14apnd-d0hir:enti typagenum=46:0:searchtype=basic.[accessed June 29, 2010], 153-155.

pastor to be more effective as a counselor.[65] Morgan's study is based on theories developed by C. G. Jung, noted Swiss psychiatrist. "The theory suggests that individuals have a dominant sexual ego-identity (male or female), which is the self-consciousness of the person. Within each person there is an element of the opposite sex. The element is identified as a *contrasexual* core, also known as the *anima* in male personalities and *animus* in females. Female pastors, in the psychic unconscious, personify the *contrasexual* masculine qualities, such as capacity to penetrate, separate, take charge, initiate, create, and stand firmly over and against, to articulate and express meaning. In male pastors, the psychic unconscious personifies the *contrasexual* feminine qualities, such as tenderness, sensitivity, deviousness, seduction, indefiniteness, feeling, receptivity, elusiveness, jealousy, creative containing, yielding and understanding."[66] This researcher felt it necessary to investigate whether the female pastors of the House of God Church possessed both qualities, which would enable them to better understand the needs of male and female. This makes sense in the vein that woman was made from man and God made both, male and female, in his likeness and image (Genesis 1:26). The image of God's spirit and soul indwelling in man is comprised of the same attributes of God in man. This is confirmed in the prayer of Christ, "That they all may be one; as thou, Father, art in me, and I in thee, that they also may be one in us: that the world may believe that thou hast sent me" (John 17:21 KJV). Nevertheless, God is not characterized totally as man, for He is divine; neither is God devious and seductive, as traits ascribed to some individuals.

---

[65] Edward Morgan, "Implications of the Masculine and the Feminine in Pastoral Ministry." *Journal of Pastoral Care* 34 no. 4 (Dec 1980): 268: 277. http://newfirstsearch.oclc.org/WebZ/FTFETCH?sessionid=fsapp6-51254-gb2iiz2q-fbvlk7:entitypagenum=243:0:rule= 100:fetchtype=fulltext:dbname =ATLA FT:recno=12:resultset=10:ftformat=PDF:format=BI:isbillable =TRUE:numrecs=1:isdirectarticle=FALSE:entityemailfullrecno=12:entityemailfullresultset=10:entityemailftfrom=ATLA FT: [accessed June 30, 2010]

[66] Morgan, 269-272.

Chapter 4 will provide results of masculine and feminine qualities of the female pastor's in this study.

The reliability and validity of the Holy Scriptures support answers to questions number one and two: "No, God is not sexist;" and "Yes, women have served as leaders from the beginning during patriarchal times." We will now investigate question number three, the role already defined in the Bible for the husbands of female leaders such as pastors, bishops, and overseers in chapter 2, part II.

Part II: Theological Analysis of Women's and Men's Roles in Leadership and Ministry

Biblical Case Studies of Female Leaders in Ministry and the Role of Their Husbands

An analysis of biblical couples and the roles of husband and wife will be analyzed in this section. Primary attention will be focused on the husband's role. This information will be used to compare with recommendations from the male spouses in the House of God Church in chapter 3.

The findings from case studies of four biblical couples will be discussed: Deborah and Lapidoth (Barak); Huldah and Shallum; Mary and Joseph; and Priscilla and Aquila. These women played integral roles in God's plan of salvation with their husbands in support of what they were commissioned to do by God. The roles of these biblical couples shall validate the roles of male spouses for further consideration in the House of God Church for generations to come.

The Case Study of Deborah and Lapidoth (Barak): Judges 4-5

Among all the women leaders in the Bible, Deborah appears to be the most abundant in courage and wisdom during her day. Two full chapters of a hermeneutical narrative are given over to Deborah, more than any other woman in the Bible. Several authors provide insights on Deborah, her husband Lapidoth, and Barak.

In Judges chapters 4-5, we have a narrative account of Deborah. The name *Deborah* means *eloquent; an orator;* and *bee.* She was the only female among the judges who served as a judge and a prophetess (Samuel was also a judge and prophet). All of the judges were military leaders except Deborah, who commissioned Barak to the position to lead the Israeli army.

The book of Judges provides historical context of the period which extended from the Exodus to the anointing of King Saul over the United Kingdom (1350 to 1050 BC). It was an era when the Israelites rejected God by sinning through disobedience. As a result, they were oppressed by the Canaanites, whom they had allowed to remain after the conquest against God's commands. It was an era of spiritual decline and political unrest. God chose particular men and women during this pre-monarchial period to rule as judges over His people. Deborah was one of the prominent females God anointed to judge all of Israel.

The exegesis of this chapter reveals that Deborah was married to Lapidoth and resided in an undisclosed location between Ramah and Bethel in the mount of Ephraim. Nothing more is mentioned about her husband in the King James Version or New Revised Standard Version interpretation of Scriptures. Deborah judged the people under the "palm tree of Deborah." She is equated to a mother concerned for the welfare of her children and was identified as "a mother in Israel" in her victory song in Judges 5:7. Deborah was compelled to encourage and motivate the people to take action against King Jabin the Canaanite and his captain Sisera, who oppressed and held the Israelites in bondage for twenty years.

Barak, the son of Abinoam (a Naphtalite)[67] and commander of the Israeli army, was summoned by Deborah. She reminded him that the LORD God of Israel had commanded him to attack the Canaanites (Judges 4:6). She instructed Barak to gather ten thousand men from

---

[67]   Herbert Lockyer, *All the Men of the Bible (Two Books in One) All the Women of the Bible.* Grand Rapids, Michigan: Zondervan, 1984, 67.

Naphtali and Zebulun to fight the Canaanites, who had a hundred thousand men and nine hundred iron chariots. Barak was hesitant to go to war and would only agree if Deborah accompanied him. Barak said to her, "If thou wilt go with me, then I will go: but if thou wilt not go with me, then I will not go." Deborah responded by saying, "I will surely go with thee: notwithstanding the journey that thou takest shall not be for thine honour; for the LORD shall sell Sisera into the hand of a woman. And Deborah arose, and went with Barak to Kedesh" (Judges 4:10).

Deborah's faith in God was unwavering, and her presence and positive attitude gave Barak the courage to stand against what appeared to be impossible odds. Deborah prophesied that Israel would win the battle. However, if she went with him, the victory would be given to a woman. Needless to say, God wrought a miracle and sent a rainstorm that flooded the land. The Canaanites were defeated by the Israelites when their iron chariots were stuck in the mud and their foot soldiers were unable to advance. Sisera escaped but was killed by Jael, a Kenite woman.

In worship and praises to God, Deborah and Barak composed a "martial song" in Judges 5, which reminded the people that their God is a "God of War" who wins all battles. She addressed the victories they had won in being led out of bondage and enabled to flee Pharaoh when crossing "the Sea of Reeds"[68] which has been interpreted as the Red Sea.

Edith Deen contends that Deborah is the only woman in the Bible placed in political power by the common consent of the people. The wife of an obscure man, she awakened the people out of lethargy and was compared to Joan of Arc, who led the French to victory centuries later.[69] Deen contends that "Because the men of Israel had faltered in leadership, Deborah arose to denounce this lack of leadership and to affirm that deliverance from oppression was at hand."[70]

Herbert Lockyer characterizes Deborah as having the roles of wife, prophetess, agitator, ruler, warrior, patriot, poetess, and maternal

---

[68] Edith Deen, *All of the Women of the Bible*. New York: HarperOne, 1983, 71.
[69] Deen, 73.
[70] Deen, 70.

figure.[71] She was the wife of Lapidoth, whose name in Hebrew is in the feminine gender instead of the masculine. Some thought her husband was a weak man married to a strong-willed woman.[72] However, Lockyer believes that Lapidoth loved and admired his wife's ability and influence and that "Deborah would never have become the dazzling figure she did, if she not had the love, sympathy, advice, and encouragement of a husband who was happy to ride in the second chariot."[73]

Lockyer further elaborates on Deborah. As a prophetess (prophet: preacher, according to Nehemiah 6:7), she had the ability to discern the mind and purpose of God and declare it to others. (Old Testament prophets were the mediators between God and the people of Israel.[74]) She was an agitator because she stirred up and excited public discussion in favor of going to war. She was a ruler, the fifth judge of Israel, whom God raised up to deliver his people. She was a patriot, warrior, and writer: a warrior because she fought with words when Barak acknowledged that he would not go to war without her. Barak had ten thousand men, and Sisera had a hundred thousand fighters and nine hundred iron chariots, but Deborah was the one who possessed the war-like spirit of patriotism.[75] Deborah was a poetess. In Judges 5, she praises the Lord, who enabled them to win the battle. She sat under the "palm tree of Deborah" located between Bethel and Ramah in the hill country of mount Ephraim; being unique and strong-minded, she counseled the people of God.[76] All of Israel was under her jurisdiction. During those days of patriarchy, women were subordinate to men, but God used her in a leadership position, and so men were subordinate to her. After the war, she ruled with peace for forty years. She was a maternal figure,

[71] Lockyer, 40-42.
[72] Lockyer, 40.
[73] Lockyer, 41.
[74] Ibid.
[75] Lockyer, 42.
[76] Lockyer, 40.

"a mother in Israel" according to Judges 5:7. It is unknown if she became a natural mother.[77]

The Richards' speak of the need for a bold, courageous, and tenacious Deborah who inspired Israel at a time of spiritual stagnation.[78] Israel repeatedly revolved in a cycle of national sin, servitude, supplication, and salvation.[79] In other words, after they sinned, God allowed them to be oppressed by the Canaanites. God had commanded that they be destroyed and not be allowed to remain in Canaan. After suffering for a long period of time, they would cry to the Lord in repentance for deliverance, and He would save them from their dreadful situation. Deborah was an unusual, charismatic leader who emerged in a time of great distress to lead God's people spiritually and politically.[80]

Deborah's relationships with God, her husband, the Israelites, and Barak are addressed by the Richardses. Her relationship with God is evident in her being a prophetess. She was God's spokesperson, not by heredity, but instead, she was chosen by God. He chooses whom He wills. Israel recognized that she had been called and commissioned by God.[81] Her love for God rings true in her song of thanksgiving in Judges 5.

In her relationship with her husband, she is identified as Lapidoth's wife. Israel was a patriarchal society. Women in the Old Testament era were identified by the men in whose household they lived (whether father's or husband's). The family "belonged" to the man; the woman belonged to the household.[82] Some translate "the wife of Lapidoth" to mean "a woman of valor."[83] There was no essential conflict between Deborah being a wife in a patriarchal age

77 Lockyer, 42.
78 Sue and Larry Richards, *Every Woman in the Bible.* Nashville, TN: Thomas Nelson Publishers, 1999, 92.
79 Richards, 92.
80 Ibid.
81 Richards, 93.
82 Ibid.
83 Ibid.

and being a spiritual leader.[84] Deborah's behavior as a virtuous wife led to the respect for her husband by the Israelites.[85]

In Deborah's relationship with the Israelites, she judged the people and was their acknowledged leader who solved their problems. Emil G. Hirsch et al. further explain that according to tradition of some, Deborah served as prophetess and judged God's people under the palm tree because women could not teach or judge in privacy, but had to be in the open air.[86]

Deborah's relationship with Barak involved her summoning him to be commander. He accepted only if she went with him. Barak felt inadequate to go without her. The Richardses contend that since God had called Barak, he should have placed his faith in His word. "Deborah recognized Israel's need to see Barak as a military leader and placed herself in the background."[87] Deborah attempts to give Barak credit for the song. "But while the verse credited Barak by name, the Hebrew has a feminine singular verb *vatashar*, literally 'and she sang.' This interplay suggests that while Deborah's special relationship with God made her the acknowledged leader of the Israelite tribes, her gender defined those roles of leadership in which she could function with God's blessings."[88] The authors acknowledge that Deborah's example is a reminder that God does not rule out women in leadership "solely on the basis of gender;" and neither does this indicate that every leadership position is appropriate for women (i.e. military commander).[89]

Very little is said about Deborah's relationship with her husband Lapidoth, but more about Barak. Supporting literature as to why Deborah, a married woman, would go to war with a man not her

---

[84]   Richards, 94.

[85]   Ibid.

[86]   Emil G. Hirsch, Gerson B. Levi, Solomon Schechter, and Kaufmann Kohler. "Deborah." http://www.jewishencyclopedia.com/view_friendly.jsp?artid=187&letter=D [accessed July 2, 2010], 2.

[87]   Richards, 95.

[88]   Ibid.

[89]   Ibid.

husband, especially during the times of patriarchy, led to additional investigation into works which addressed rabbinical literature. The writings of Patrick Reardon, Morris Jastrow, and Emil Hirsch et al. revealed a mystery hidden from many. Emil Hirsch et al. state that in their research of rabbinical literature, they have come to the conclusion that *Lapidoth and Barak are one and the same man.*[90] *Lapidoth* has a feminine connotation and means "the woman who furnished wicks for the lamps" for the Shiloh sanctuary. Jewish tradition states that Deborah encouraged Lapidoth, which is not his proper name, to make the lights for the sanctuary, but instead he made the lights into blazing torches.[91] "His real name was *Barak,* given to him because his face 'shone like lightning,' and he was also called Michael because he was modest before God.[92] This is an indication that the Spirit of God rests alike upon Jew and Gentile; man and woman; and bondman and bondwoman."[93] Patrick Reardon confirms the findings of Hirsch et al. that Lapidoth and Barak are one and the same man.[94] Just think—what man would allow his wife to go away with any man to battle without him to protect her personally?

Cornwall states that *Lapidoth* means *torches,* i.e. having eyes of fire; enlightened; lightning flashes (root) 1) a torch; 2) a lamp; 3) a flame, to shine, and flames.[95] Jastrow contends that Lapidoth was small in stature before the war, or a small light, or *lappidot,* a pious and ignorant man. However, after Israel conquered Sisera's army, he (Barak) was a big light.[96] Accordingly, Deborah suggested to Barak to make candles to be offered by him for the sanctuary of Shiloh in an effort to serve God. Therefore, she was known as "the wife of Lapidoth." Jewish tradition says Lapidoth/Barak was a student of Joshua and was one of the elders left to serve with

---

90 Jastrow, B1.
91 Ibid.
92 Jastrow, B1.
93 Hirsch, D2.
94 Patrick Henry Reardon, "Judge Deborah: The Hebrew Prophetess in Christian Tradition. *Touchstone (US)* 13 no. 3 (Ap 2000):18-25.
95 Cornwall, 158.
96 Jastrow, B1.

Deborah. It also says that he was modest, that he was the leader of the war, and that he did not mind being second place to Deborah. [97] Lockyer acknowledges that in Barak's deliverance of Israel, Deborah is mentioned first.[98] Judges 5:1-2 gives this account when they sang the praise song. The writer of Hebrews 11:32-34 commends Barak's faithfulness and obedience to Deborah, yet not brave initially:

> And what shall I more say? for the time would fail me to tell of Gedeon, and of Barak, and of Samson, and of Jephthae; of David also, and Samuel, and of the prophets: Who through faith subdued kingdoms, wrought righteousness, obtained promises, stopped the mouths of lions, quenched the violence of fire, escaped the edge of the sword, out of weakness were made strong, waxed valiant in fight, turned to flight the armies of the aliens.

Although biblical interpretations (KJV and NRSV) do not acknowledge Barak and Lapidoth as one and the same, Reardon states that in rabbinical literature, Rupert of Deutz, Andrew of St. Victor, and Peter Comoestor contend that Deborah summoned Barak (her husband) to battle.[99] Reardon styles Deborah as decisive and Barak as timid.[100] God's deliverance of Israel from her enemies was a result of Deborah's spiritual insight and wisdom as the first prophetic figure after the Exodus.[101]

Jastrow contends that we should not consider Barak's actions as degrading because Deborah is recognized for leading Israel into battle. Instead, this is an indication of Barak's respect for Deborah's position of authority and his subordinate position under her. It is worth noting that Deborah believed being a military commander was more of a man's duty than a woman's. At the end, Barak proved to be

---

[97] Ibid.

[98] Lockyer, 67.

[99] Patrick Henry Reardon,"Judge Deborah: The Hebrew Prophetess in Christian Tradition." *Touchstone (US)* 13 no. 3 (Ap 2000):18-25.

[100] Reardon, 18.

[101] Reardon, 20.

valiant and won the war with God's intervention. It is understandable why Lapidoth would be happy to ride in the second chariot, if his wife Judge Deborah was riding in the first chariot.

To summarize Lapidoth's role as Deborah's husband, it seems that he had great love for her. Lapidoth recognized that Deborah was called by God and admired her ability and influence when counseling God's people. Due to the fact that they were inseparable and worked together as a team to defeat the Canaanites, it appears that there were no feelings of insecurity or conflict, on his behalf regarding Deborah's leadership over Israel. Deborah and Lapidoth/Barak as a team were obedient to God, prayed together, waged war together, sang together, and praised God together for deliverance. Lapidoth/Barak's trust in Deborah's prophetic abilities and faith in God makes this a guide for a happy marriage. Lapidoth's life demonstrated leadership (served as military leader), mentorship (advised wife), and brotherhood (avoided patriarchal conflicts by working as a team under wife's authority). (See appendix 1.)

The Case Study of Huldah and Shallum: 2 Kings 22:14-20; 2 Chronicles 34:22-33

According to Lockyer, Huldah is a prophetess who served during the reign of King Josiah. She was married to Shallum. When the lost Book of the Law was found, King Josiah sent the book to Huldah to verify its authenticity. This led to the repentance of the king, who then began a religious revival. Huldah prophesized judgment on the disobedient nation, and as the result of King Josiah's tender heart, humility, and faithfulness to God, he died in peace. After his death, Judah was invaded by the Babylonians.[102] Interestingly enough, Josiah listened to the prophetic words of Huldah regarding the future destruction that would come as a result of the nation's idolatry. He obeyed God by destroying the groves and idols the Hebrews were worshipping.

---

[102]   Lockyer, 69-70.

Huldah means *weasel, endurance,* and *perpetuity.*[103] Huldah the prophetess is noted for saying, "Thus saith the Lord." This is an indication of her trust, faithfulness, and commitment and her attentive ear to listen to what God had to say, according to Larry and Sue Richards.[104]

Huldah was also a teacher. Evidently, she was the only one in the kingdom capable of identifying the lost book known as the Book of Deuteronomy.[105] Scripture reveals she lived in the college located in Jerusalem. According to Jewish tradition, Huldah taught publicly in a school or second quarter in front of the Temple; others claim she taught and preached to women.[106] Easton states that the second quarter was considered the suburb of the city, between the inner and outer walls.[107]

Deen asserts that Huldah most likely was consulted by Josiah instead of a man because of his closeness to his mother, Queen Jedidah. However, due to the fact that Josiah's mother was godly, he may have been more sympathetic to righteous women.[108] Josiah's father Ammon was killed by his servants when Josiah was a youth. Hirsch et al, on the one hand, claim that Huldah was related to Jeremiah (descendants by marriage of Rahab and Joshua), who preached during this era. Jeremiah preached to the men, and Huldah preached to the women.[109] However, it is possible that Huldah did teach to some men because the college was where the sons of the prophets met to study God's word and to receive the instructions of their teachers.[110]

---

[103] Cornwall, 107.

[104] Richards, 147-148.

[105] Ibid.

[106] Deen, 144.

[107] Matthew Easton, "Deborah." Edited by Paul S. Taylor. http://www.christiananswers.net/dictionary/deborah.html [accessed July 2, 2010], 1.

[108] Deen, 144-145.

[109] Emil G. Hirsch, M. Seligsohn, Executive Committee of the Editorial Board, and Louis Ginzberg. "Huldah" http://www.jewishencyclopedia.com/view_friendly.jsp?artid=955&letter=H [accessed July 2, 2010],1.

[110] John Wesley Explanatory Notes. http://www.christnotes.org/commentary.php?com=wes&b=12&c=22.

As a result, Huldah rightly divided the word of truth and was prophetic, as well as being a righteous woman who prophesied to Judah. She had a reputation for being God's spokesperson. The Richardses claim that Habakkuk was living during this time period, but the king chose to use Huldah.[111] Both 2 Kings and 2 Chronicles honor her as a prophetess and a wife. As it was said about Deborah, Huldah was able to balance her responsibilities as prophetess, wife, and teacher. There was no conflict between her religious responsibilities and her wifely duties. Her prophesying and Josiah's public readings of the law brought about a revival in the nation.[112] She shall be remembered as being intelligent and wise—an educator, religious leader, and prophetess.

Shallum was the son of Tikvah and husband of Huldah, whose name means *retribution, recompense, spoliation, rewarder, requital,* and *restitution.*[113] Hitchocks says the name *Shallum* means *perfect, agreeable.*[114] Not much is written about him with the exception that Shallum's family were "keepers of the wardrobe." The family members, most likely, were responsible for the maintenance of the priest's garments.

As an employee in the temple, Shallum supported his wife and trusted in her spiritual wisdom. Huldah's ministry was not a threat to him as a man, nor as a professional serving in the temple. His love for God and his wife was evident in the occupations they shared in ministry. Shallum was not intimidated by Huldah's position over him, but he understood her calling from the true and living God. Shallum evidently avoided patriarchal conflict because he was peaceable. He did not try to interfere with the revival or Huldah's prophetic ministry. Shallum and Huldah both working in the temple, most likely, led to their close relationships with the king and priests. Shallum trusted in his wife's wisdom and knew her prophecies came from God. Shallum's life demonstrated leadership (held a prestigious

[111] Richards, 147-148.
[112] Ibid.
[113] Cornwall, 213.
[114] "Hitchcock's Dictionary of Bible Names": Shallum. http://www.christnotes.org/dictionary.php? dict=hbn&id=2206.

position in the temple), mentorship (advised wife), and brotherhood (avoided patriarchal conflicts). (See appendix 1.)

The Case Study of Mary and Joseph: Matthew 1:16-24; 2:13; Luke 1-3

Mary, a young virgin of Nazareth, was the spouse of Joseph. She was from the tribe of Judah, lineage of David. Dake notes that she was a descendant of Nathan, David's oldest son (2 Samuel 5:14; Luke 1:32), and Heli was her father.[115] *Mary* has numerous meanings: *bitterness, rebellious, obstinate* (root: trouble, sorrow, disobedience; rebellion). *Mary* is also the Greek form of *Miriam,* meaning *their rebellion.*[116] Lockyer says *Mary* means *super-eminence, selection, sanctity, submission, salutation, service,* and *sorrow.*[117] Based on the narratives of Mary's journey, the meanings of her name describe the emotions she experienced during her lifetime.

Not much is revealed in Scripture concerning Mary; however, when she was engaged to Joseph, the angel Gabriel appeared to her and said she was "highly favored and blessed among women" (Luke 1:28) and that, through the power of God, she would conceive a son named Jesus, who would be Savior of the world. Mary questioned her ability to have a child when she was chaste. Mary's faith and trust in God led her to humbly accept God's will, and she said, " . . . be it unto me according to thy word" (Luke 1:38). In spite of the fact that Mary was not a prophetess, she was predestined in eternity to carry "the Holy Seed," Jesus Christ, for nine months in her womb. She continues to be highly honored today among mankind.

Mary pondered in her heart the many acts and words of Jesus. She supported Jesus and followed Him as He traveled His earthly

---

[115] Finis Jennings Dake, *Dake's Annotated Reference Bible: The Holy Bible.* Lawrenceville, GA: Dake Publishing Co., Second Printing October 2007, 106.

[116] Cornwall, 167.

[117] Lockyer, 92-98.

journey, unto His death. She was present when Jesus performed His first miracle (John 1:1-10) and at the foot of the cross at His crucifixion (John 19:25-27). She shared the good news of the Messiah with others. Mary was in the upper room and received the Holy Ghost with the other disciples and women (Acts 1:13-14; 2:1-4), as promised. This is an indication of everyone needing the Holy Ghost in order to live a righteous life. Youngblood et al. proclaim of Mary, "As the first member of the human race to accept Christ, she stands as the first of the redeemed and as the flagship of humanity itself. She is our enduring example for faith, service to God, and a life of righteousness."[118]

Joseph means *may God add, he shall add,* and *increasing.*[119] Joseph, a Nazarite, was from the tribe of Judah, the lineage of David, a descendant of his son Solomon (Matthew 1:6-16). Mary and Joseph were of the Davidic line united by Zerubbabel and the marriage of Salathiel to Neri's daughter of Nathan's line.[120] Joseph was not the natural father of Jesus, but His step-father. Jesus, born of the Virgin Mary, is the son of God. However, Joseph gained legal rights to the Davidic throne according to the Jewish law of blood-rights. The Scripture says Joseph is the "son" of Heli. Dake says the true interpretation means Joseph is "the son-in-law" of Heli, who was Mary's father (Luke 3:23); Joseph's birth father was Jacob.[121] According to Dake, women were not named as heads of households in genealogies, and Joseph's name represented Mary.[122] Edith Deen acknowledges Joseph as Jesus' only legal father, a humble and industrious laborer (carpenter), protector of Mary, the legal guardian and provider of Jesus, kindly and good, and one who loved Mary.[123]

---

[118] R. F. Youngblood, Herbert Lockyer Sr., F. F. Bruce, and R. K. Harrison, eds., *Nelson's New Illustrated Bible Dictionary.* Nashville: Thomas Nelson Publishers,1995, 806.

[119] Cornwall, 149.

[120] Dake, 106.

[121] Dake, 105-106.

[122] Dake, 105.

[123] Deen, 161-162.

Sue and Larry Richards state that Mary was about thirteen years of age when she married Joseph, who was an older man.[124] "Joseph was sensitive and fair because he considered divorce during the betrothal period, but he did not divorce her. He was not vindictive, although he was hurt when Mary became with child. Joseph demonstrated that he was a man of faith when the angel Gabriel told him Mary had not been unfaithful. Joseph did not think about his own reputation; neither was he concerned that the community thought that they committed fornication before the wedding. Joseph loved and trusted God and was willing to obey Him. Despite disparity of age, they were well matched."[125] Mary and Joseph were well-adjusted in their marriage and had eight children: four sons and four daughters (Matthew 13:55; John 7:3-5). Joseph was not jealous of Mary's close relationship with Jesus, but was caring and honorable.

Lockyer says Joseph was present at the birth of Jesus. He was a praying and patient man who waited upon God. His love for Mary and Jesus was so immense that her not bearing his child did not alter his love for them. To avoid embarrassment, the angel spoke to Joseph regarding God's plan and instructed him to take Mary as his wife because the child was of holy conception. Joseph obeyed and trusted God. When King Herod searched for the baby Jesus to kill and had other baby boys under two years of age slaughtered in the process, Joseph's love for Jesus was so intense that, being directed by God, he protected his family by fleeing to Egypt until the king's death.

Joseph was a pious Israelite and faithful in all the ordinances of the temple (Luke 2:22-24, 41-42). He could have claimed royalty because he was of the priestly descent as "a son of David" (Matthew 1:20). However, due to his humbleness, he preferred being like any ordinary, charitable man (Luke 2:1-7; Matthew 1:19). Joseph was an industrious, self-employed carpenter who taught his son his trade.[126] According to tradition, he died at age 111 when Jesus

[124] Richards, 169-174.
[125] Richards, 171.
[126] Lockyer, 123.

was 18 years old and became "a son of the Law" (Luke 2:41-51).[127] In conclusion, Joseph was obedient to God and believed in God's purpose for his wife. Joseph was caring and faithful to Mary and protective of the family he loved. His life demonstrates leadership (industrious, self-employed), mentorship (taught Christ the carpentry trade), and brotherhood (adopted his wife's son born of God). (See appendix 1.)

The Case Study of Priscilla and Aquilla: Acts 18:2, 18, 26; Romans 16:3

Priscilla and Aquila were a married couple who worked as a team in ministry. As Jewish converts, they lived in Rome until they were forced to leave by Claudius (Acts 18:2). Priscilla is a diminutive of *Prisca*, meaning *ancient, little old woman; hence worthy, venerable*.[128] She was an influential Jewess. This husband and wife teaching team is always named together in ministry. Priscilla is named first three times, while Aquila is named first only once in Scripture. Sue and Larry Richards indicate that Priscilla being named first by Paul is an indication that her spiritual gifts and contributions at least equaled those of her husband.[129]

Edith Deen contends that Priscilla and Aquila were influential teachers of Christianity; they were studious and religious, and they also demonstrated practical ability as tent-makers in Corinth and Ephesus.[130] The couple traveled with Paul to Syria, where he left them in charge in Ephesus (Acts 18:18-19). They organized a mission there while Paul was in Syria for a year.[131]

Paul called her Prisca, which indicates a close relationship between him and the couple.[132] Evidently, Aquila was secure and

---

[127] Lockyer, 202-204.
[128] Cornwall, 198.
[129] Richards, 207.
[130] Deen, 227.
[131] Deen, 227-230.
[132] Deen, 228.

trusting in the relationship the couple shared with Paul and was not jealous. Priscilla was able to balance her roles as a wife, a homemaker, and a career woman as a tent weaver. Her husband supported her endeavors. In her missionary efforts, she had a zeal for Christ and saw the need to help her fellow man. Scripture indicates how Priscilla expounded to Apollos a more perfect way of God (Acts 18:26).

Aquila in Hebrew means *I shall be nourished;* in Latin, *eagle;* and in Greek, *immovable.*[133] Priscilla may have been named first primarily because she perhaps became a believer before her husband, according to Dinsdale Young.[134] They were a team who were inseparable in spirit, mind, and body.

"The oneness of Priscilla and Aquila is expressed as being one in marital bliss; . . . their love for each other was expressed in them being inseparable . . . They were righteous and one in the Lord . . . The couple possessed a Holy zeal in witnessing for Christ and service to the church by having a church in their homes at Ephesus and Rome . . . They were partners in faithful endeavors; and one in secular occupation as tentmakers . . . As honest business persons, they established a reputation of being witnesses for Christ . . . One in friendship as demonstrated in their relationship with Paul as co-laborers."[135] Lockyer states that when they were not teaching and preaching, they supported themselves making tents. Jewish tradition states that rabbis taught that fathers were to teach their children a trade so they would not become thieves.[136]

Marie Keller states that Priscilla and Aquila encouraged, supported, and challenged each other because they knew each other's gifts and strengths and made the most of them.[137] Interpreters such as John Chrysostom suggest that Priscilla's name appearing first signifies that she was the main teacher of Apollos.[138] Keller's findings indicate issues of subordination were not present in Priscilla's relationships with her

---

[133] Cornwall, 18.

[134] Lockyer, 122.

[135] Lockyer, 122-125.

[136] Lockyer, 123.

[137] Marie Noël Keller, *Priscilla and Aquila: Paul's Coworkers in Christ Jesus.* Collegeville, Minnesota: Liturgical Press, 2010, 65.

[138] Keller, 65.

husband Aquila or Paul. This is noteworthy to consider because they resided in the male-dominated society of the Greco-Roman world. It is evident that she was considered an equal. Keller states that Priscilla teaches us the importance of women's equal leadership.[139]

In conclusion, this husband and wife team loved together, worked together, and witnessed together for Christ's sake. It is unknown if they died together in Rome as martyrs for the gospel of Jesus Christ. Their model for team ministry is an excellent example for couples in ministry that co-pastor, as well as an excellent model for the roles of Christian husbands and wives in ministry. Indeed, Aquila was faithful to God and his wife. He obeyed God, and he was trusting, righteous, and secure in supporting his wife in ministry. Aquila's life demonstrated the skills of leadership (co-pastor, missionary, businessman); brotherhood (businessman, trustworthy); and mentorship (teaching). (See appendix 1.)

Summary of the Role of Biblical Husbands

It is noteworthy to consider that these four women (Deborah, Huldah, Mary, and Priscilla) were women that left a legacy to be admired and followed by women called by God. These anointed, strong-willed, and tenacious women of God were married to men of God who were obedient to the voice and direction of the Almighty, and who in their own right were leaders.

The chart in appendix 1 depicts the role of each female leader's husband individually. The following commonalities of the four husbands (Lapidoth/Barak, Shallum, Joseph, and Aquila) are noted:

- Obedient to God
- Avoided patriarchal conflicts by allowing the wife to fulfill her calling by God
- Believed in God and His purpose for his wife
- Did not interfere with his wife's ministerial vocation
- Industrious by being gainfully employed

---

[139]   Keller, 73.

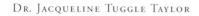

- Faithful to God and his wife
- Loved his wife
- Respected his wife's relationship with God and man
- Supported his wife
- Faithful in church attendance
- Communicated with God
- Demonstrated leadership skills

There is no doubt that what God joins together, no man should put asunder. Man and woman are complete and make a whole. Saved married couples who are called by God into a vocation of ministry are ideal. What the world needs to sow is seeds of love, peace, and joy. When married couples are in the will of God, their mission on earth is possible with His help. The roles of these biblical women's husbands have clearly been defined by Scripture for us to use as a pattern of good works.

ETHNOGRAPHIC TOOLS
AND METHODOLOGY

Part I: Methodology Description
and Purpose of Brief Pastoral Counseling

Chapter 3 describes the context of this study and its purpose. The methodology employed for this project to answer the question of the female pastor's husband's role will be based on those developed by Howard Stone in his book *The Strategies of Brief Counseling*. The survey and interview questions serve as tools for a pastoral counselor to utilize when feasible in attempting to resolve issues of conflict. Individuals who do not know their role in life will often have unnecessary stress or tension in their lives. The survey questionnaires were distributed to fifteen men to ascertain their perception of how they viewed their roles as husbands to pastors in the church. In-depth interviews followed with husbands willing to participate. Guidelines for the role of the female pastor's husband will be analyzed from the responses of these men. The findings of this study will be presented in a seminar comprised of clergy and laity and will be titled "The Role of the Female Pastor's Husband." The goal of utilizing brief counseling strategies is to have the husbands participate in developing their role as the pastor's husband; in so doing, they will be able to resolve issues which possibly have been a concern in their life.

This chapter explains the strategies of brief pastoral counseling, how the survey and interview questions were formulated, and how they were used to collect data for analysis and evaluation. Masculine and feminine characteristics of pastors as presented by Edward Morgan were used to develop questions. This chapter also discusses how these questions were linked to the research project and elements of brief pastoral counseling strategies while providing validity and reliability to the results of the project.

As previously expressed, one goal of this project is to have the participants become stakeholders in defining their role as "first gentleman" in the House of God Church. In life, man will be confronted with problems; however, as the book of Proverbs suggests, counsel (advice) will often be needed: "Where no counsel is, the people fall: but in the multitude of counselors there is safety" (Proverbs 11:14, KJV). Some men desire to hear directly from God, their Supreme Being, for directions. On the other hand, others desire to use individuals to help guide them in the appropriate directions when they are unsure which actions to take. The methodology used in this study is one that a pastoral counselor may use in aiding a client to solve a problem. In this particular case, the husbands are seeking to define their own roles.

Many people believe that counselors are viewed as agents of God and serve as guides on His behalf. As the researcher (counselor) who will interview the first husbands (counselees), I will use Howard Stone's strategies of brief pastoral counseling in the methodology to develop questions for this study.[140] The responses to these questions will provide conclusions that describe the role of the female pastor's husband. The works of others in counseling have been an influence in determining which approach is best to use in these one-on-one counseling sessions and in developing survey and interview questions. Works of other noted scholars (Pamela Cooper-White, Edward Wimberly, and Robert Dykstra) served as prerequisites before interviewing the husbands. The personalities of these husbands were taken into consideration before, during, and after the interview counseling session.

---

[140] Howard W. Stone, ed., *Strategies for Brief Pastoral Counseling*. Minneapolis: Fortress Press, 2001, 91-103.

The brief pastoral counseling theory was selected for this study because it may be *individually focused*.[141] Only husbands are being interviewed, as opposed to couples. This will allow them to define their individual role. Howard Stone, editor, presents the brief pastoral counseling strategies employed in this study and concludes that brief pastoral counseling is a process that aides the pastor in envisioning the best aspects of pastoral care for the counselee. Most of the questions in the surveys and interviews given to the husbands were based on ten elements suggested by Stone.

Brief Counseling Strategies Theory

Dr. Howard W. Stone, during the publication of *Strategies for Brief Pastoral Counseling,* was the professor of psychology and pastoral counseling at Brite Divinity School at Texas Christian University in Fort Worth, Texas.

The brief pastoral counseling elements are: (1) brief orientation; (2) empathic relationship; (3) solvable focal problem; (4) assessment; (5) exceptions; (6) limited goals; (7) a plan; (8) active counseling; (9) achievable homework; and (10) building on strengths.[142] Stone quotes Amos 3:3 (NIV): "Can two walk together unless they agree?"[143] The counselor and counselee must establish a rapport with one another. A brief synopsis of the ten elements will be discussed below.[144]

Brief orientation encompasses a four-fold purpose. (1) It maintains that the counselor may only see the person one time because the counselee may not return; (2) the counselor does not attempt to "fix" all of the individual's problems; (3) it attempts to avoid dependency on the counselor by the counselee; and (4) it guides the counselee in recognizing that good and bad exist in this world and that the counselee must look to God, in faith, for all things.[145] To further

---

[141] Stone, 91.

[142] Stone, 91.

[143] Stone, 107.

[144] Stone, 91.

[145] Stone, 92.

explain brief orientation, the pastoral counselor must realize that the number of sessions scheduled is not the primary focus when caring for the counselee. Instead, what is of utmost importance is the care the counselor provides and the interventions to be employed. The session must be brief because there is never a guarantee that a counselee will return after the initial visit; therefore, the counselor must, with simplicity, resolve the problem at hand. Therefore, the counselor must value every moment and take advantage of the opportunity to provide the best care to the counselee during the counseling session. The goal of the counselor is to motivate the counselee to face the realities of life, with its challenges, issues, and concerns, by being faithful and trusting in God while using his or her "God-given" abilities to resolve the problems he or she can.

Stone emphasizes the significance of establishing an empathic relationship with the counselee. This builds trust with the counselee; it will guide the counselor in knowing which interventions to employ. It will also give the counselor the ability to recognize that the counselee is the authority on what his or her problems and solutions are and to remember that we are mere instruments of peace.[146] Immediately establishing a rapport will allow the counselee to feel accepted; therefore, the counselor must be willing to hear what the counselee has to say. This will open the door for the counselee to be willing to cooperate when change is necessary.[147] Counselors are responsible for demonstrating attentiveness to verbal and nonverbal clues from the counselee, while suspending judgment and being respectful to the counselee's opinions.

Stone presents a plan to *hear, fit, watch, and wait* when conducting brief counseling sessions face to face.[148] Counselors must listen attentively, which establishes rapport with the counselees, who in turn will feel that their emotions are respected and are accepted and heard.[149] The pastoral responses must fit those being counseled.

---

[146]   Stone, 92-93.

[147]   Stone, 92.

[148]   Stone, 106-108.

[149]   Stone, 107.

Counselors are to watch, listen, and wait. First, watch or look for God's activity in the counselee's life. Second, listen for the counselee to tell you how God has been active in his personal story and how he has noticed how others have treated him as a pastor's husband. Third, wait for a shift of past practices to new solutions offered by the counselee in building rapport with the counselor.

A successful brief counseling experience is necessary. Begin the session with clear, specific, and concrete goals when identifying a solvable focal problem. It is therefore essential to guide the counselee to focus on the key problem(s).[150] Staying focused on the problem for the specific visit eliminates spending unnecessary time on unimportant issues. The key issue is, "What is this man's role as the pastor's husband?"

To the pastoral counselor, diagnosis and treatment of an individual are not needed for this study. What is needed is to consider what the counselee needs to resolve the problem. Assessment and change-oriented activities should occur simultaneously during the brief counseling sessions.[151] Change should begin immediately during the first interview.[152] The process of assessment continues until the termination of the last session with the counselee. It involves observation of the behavior of the counselee and his interaction with others. Once the counselee has resolved the problem, a change in behavior will be manifested.[153]

Stone states that several questions should be asked of the counselee during assessment. The counseling session is to interview individuals so they can express concerns for their roles as husbands of female pastors, and not because they are being counseled for a medical or mental condition. Assessment in this case is determined by the participants providing definitive roles for themselves as husbands of female pastors.

The role of the female pastor's husband is the exception to the rule that "only men should pastor or become bishops," as explained in

---

[150]   Stone, 93.

[151]   Stone, 94.

[152]   Ibid.

[153]   Stone, 94.

chapter 2. Many of these men may not have viewed this as a problem before and perhaps never complained about the issue or just viewed their position concerning the topic as unimportant. In brief pastoral counseling, it is situations such as this that are of primary importance and become the focus for this session. Asking who, what, where, when, and how will aid in discovering the exceptions to the problem.

The undefined role of the first husband may be primarily the "root" or exception to the existence of stress, poor health, and a lack of communication in the marriage, which are secondary. Giving the counselee homework, such as "Think of how you would like the role of the female pastor's husband to be defined," may very well stimulate the husband in recognizing that a change in roles may give others a new perspective on his position and hopefully give the husband a new outlook on life. This will build his self-esteem and evoke interest in knowing that the husband's role changes from being the exception to becoming the goal of counseling.[154]

The need for limited targeted goals is preceded by the prerequisites of defining a specific and concrete problem and discovering the exception to that problem.[155] It does a counselor good not to be inundated with problem analysis, but through "countertransference"[156] (having the ability to empathize with another based on personal experiences), the counselor can help the counselee seek a solution to the problem.

This element is especially significant to this project because it assists in getting individuals who will only be surveyed or interviewed once in their response. It is best to be specific in obtaining the information needed for this study by asking future questions (such as "How would you like for your role to be defined a year from now?"[157]) or asking a "miracle question" (such as "How might your life be different if you, as well as others, knew to the point what

---

[154]   Stone, 96.

[155]   Ibid.

[156]   Pamela Cooper-White, *Shared Wisdom: The Use of the Self in Pastoral Care and Counseling.* Minneapolis: Augsburg Fortress, 2004, 9.

[157]   Stone, 96.

your role entailed?"). Stone offers a variety of questions to be asked that specifically target the subject, "What is your role right now?"[158] Scaling or coping questions also open the door to the counselee's honest opinion by asking, "On a scale of one to ten, what would you do to change how you are perceived in your present role as the pastor's husband?"[159]

In the initial brief counseling session, the counselor's task is to help the counselee visualize what the future will be like once the problem is resolved. Another approach is to ask miracle questions by having the counselee look at the problem in the past tense as opposed to the present.[160]

It is the responsibility of the counselor to assist the counselee in developing an achievable plan that is clear and concise, has as few steps as possible, and attains objectives within a reasonable time frame (preferably in hours or a few days) that will effect positive change. The plan is a motivating factor for change and growth. When signed by the counselee, the plan is an indication of his or her commitment to an attainable goal.[161] When man realizes that God has a plan and purpose for each of us, he will be encouraged to modify his life when and where necessary. Jeremiah 29:11 (NIV) says, "'For I know the plans I have for you,' declares the LORD, 'plans of peace to prosper you and not to harm you, plans to give you hope and a future.'"

Active counseling involves the counselor being proactive in collaborating with the counselee in providing interventions to the goals primarily established by them. Passivity on the part of the counselor only prolongs remediation of the problem. This motivates the participant to be willing to actively engage in conversation.

Achievable homework is synonymous with "outside-of-sessions tasks."[162] It is important for the counselee to be able to effect change

---

[158]   Ibid.
[159]   Stone, 97-98.
[160]   Stone, 97.
[161]   Stone, 99.
[162]   Stone, 100.

in real life by actively completing a task to reinforce the set goal for the session. Making it real affords the counselee opportunities for self-help by bringing a solution to the problem. The counselee will make a determination of his role.

Stone contends that the words of Henry Emerson Fosdick[163] express his philosophy in the healing of the counselee: "The human soul at its best experiences invading spiritual forces which can transform, illumine, direct, and empower life."[164] Gerkins states that the human document[165] (mankind) will experience conditions in life that will cause pain and discouragement. Individuals must build on strengths. Individuals are not always cognizant of their inner strengths. Counselees must be motivated to "stir up the gift that is within" according to the apostle Paul's instructions to Pastor Timothy: "Wherefore I put thee in remembrance that thou stir up the gift of God, which is in thee by the putting on of my hands" (2 Timothy 1:6). Brief pastoral counseling strategies help the counselee realize that it is his or her latent strengths that build self-esteem. In order to bring awareness to the counselee, he or she must feel welcomed, encouraged, and complimented for the positive things he or she is doing, as opposed to past wrongs.[166] The apostle Paul encourages the church of Ephesus in Ephesians 3:20 concerning the God we serve with these eloquent, powerful words: "Now unto him that is able to do exceeding abundantly above all that we ask or think, according to the power that worketh in us . . . ." Stone reminds us not to coerce anyone to share his or her problem, although he or she seeks your help; we are to respect the other person's privacy and any unwillingness to discuss a matter.

Counselors must be reminded that brief pastoral counseling is as effective as long-range counseling sessions. The elements presented by Stone provide a process that takes less time, yet is ethical, respects of the needs of the counselee, and enables the counselee to build self-

---

163   Ibid.
164   Ibid.
165   Stone/Gerkins, 100.
166   Stone, 101.

esteem with faith in God. The responses given will relate directly to the question of this study: "What is the role of the female pastor's husband in the House of God Church?"

This theory is especially beneficial to both counselor and counselee because it provides a venue for open and honest discussions regarding the role of the first husband. Most importantly, the counselee is not threatened by his response to the counselor; this allows him to place acceptance and confidence in the counselor, so that the goal of ascertaining the appropriate responses is achieved.

Instrumentation/Formation of Survey and Interview Questions

Several ethnographic tools and methods were utilized in this study. The survey and interview questions were primarily formulated based on observations of the female pastors and their spouses, the review of literature, and personal experiences as a married female pastor. A field journal was used to document observations of "first gentlemen" in worship, communion, missionary work, and other evangelistic endeavors with their wives and to note if there were changes in motivation. Eight interviews with the respondents took place at an agreed location. The interview questionnaire used consisted primarily of open-ended questions in order to obtain honest responses to the research question. The respondents did not agree to use an audio recorder, tapes, nor video during the interviews. Culmination of this research project will be in a seminar where we can share, discuss findings, make adjustments, and celebrate transformation.

How Survey and Interview Questions Linked to Research

The elements of brief pastoral counseling strategies were used to link the development of a survey questionnaire (see appendix 2) and an interview questionnaire (see appendix 3). The respondents' answers were recorded in a grid for data organization (see appendix 4). Since there will be only one interview, the value of the limited time with the counselee of no more than one and one-half hours, has been taken into consideration. Questions were direct, to the point, and open-ended in order to obtain the necessary information needed for this study, which is, "What is the role of the female pastor's husband in the House of God Church, Pentecostal Holiness denomination?"

Survey questions one through nine concerned demographics and were not based on Stone's theory.

Demographics:

1. Age
2. Race
3. What denomination were you before you married the pastor?
4. How long have you been married to the pastor?
5. Was your wife a pastor before you were married?
6. How many years have you been married?
7. Have you been married previously?
8. Do you have school-age children?
9. What is your occupation?

Brief Counseling Strategies for Survey Form

Questions ten through fifteen on the survey form were developed based on the following assumptions of Dr. Stone's elements for brief pastoral counseling strategies:

Assessment
10. How would you describe your role as the pastor's husband?

Empathic Relationship and Solvable Focal Problem
11. What are your wife's expectations of you in the church?
12. What are the members' expectations of you as the pastor's husband?

Building on Strengths
13. What do you like best about being the pastor's husband?

Limited Goals
14. What do you least like about being the pastor's husband?

Active Counseling/A Plan
15. What further training or experience do you think is needed to better prepare you in your role as the pastor's husband?

Questions for the interview questionnaire were also developed based on the brief counseling strategies as presented by Dr. Stone. Some questions may fall under more than one category. The number on the Interview form falls under the specific categories as following (for example, question #8 on the Interview form demonstrates **empathetic relationship**:

Brief Counseling Strategies for Interview Form

1. What other positions do you hold in the church presently?

Empathetic Relationship
8. Have you discussed the role of the 1st husband with other 1st husbands in other denominations? If so, how did they describe their role?
9. Have you discussed the role of the 1st husband with other 1st husbands in the House of God Church? If so, how did they describe their role?

Solvable Focal Problem
3. How do you differentiate your roles as Pastor's husband, husband, and member?

Assessment/Exceptions
6. What is your perception of the role of the Pastor's husband presently?

Limited Goals
7. Are there barriers of being a 1st husband? If so, explain what they are.

A Plan/Achievable Homework

10. How would you define the role of the Pastor's husband for future considerations?

Active Counseling

4. Have you mentored (counseled or given advice to) anyone in the church? (Also Building on Strengths)

Building on Strengths

2. What programs have you instituted in the church in your role as Pastor's husband?

5. What is your theological belief concerning female pastors and bishops? What scriptures may come to mind to support your belief?

These specific questions were developed so that participants would identify their roles as first husbands. The outcomes were to identify certain tasks and address areas of leadership, mentorship, and brotherhood as characteristics of the first husband's role as suggested by Mr. Wright[167] and Dr. Daniel.[168]

Most importantly, the counselee is building self-esteem and is an integral part in resolving his problem in knowing his role. The counselee is the one who actually defines his role as first husband or "first gentleman" by focusing on a solvable problem and by outlining a structured plan to achieve his goal. Change is likely to occur in the way the counselee performs tasks in the future, when others recognize the change as the process of brief counseling strategies being unfolded.

During active counseling, it was determined, after interviewing three of the respondents, that it was difficult to obtain more specific information concerning their role. Additional questions were developed to gain in-depth information. Studies by Edward Morgan

---

[167] Wright, 12.
[168] Daniel, 29-30.

were introduced as a part of the methodology to determine if the female pastors possessed feminine and masculine characteristics.

The husbands were presented with the following checklist that concerned characteristics their wives possessed, based on Morgan's study.[169] The husbands were then asked to provide a phrase or word that would best describe their wives. Additional questions were added to the interview questionnaire to garner a more open dialogue. It was interesting that none of the men wanted to answer question E: "Based on a scale of one to ten (1-10), would you change how you are perceived in your present role as the pastor's husband? If yes, what number would you choose?" The response from the men when asked, "Why did you refuse to answer the question?" was that they did not know how they are presently perceived by others. Also, for questions B, C, and F the men asked for further clarification of the questions; therefore, that information was provided in a way that would not influence their responses. They were all honest and straightforward and thoroughly enjoyed being an integral part of history in the making, even in their anonymity.

Additional Interview Questions

A. Which of the following characteristics describes your wife? Check all that apply.

1. Tenderness (gentleness, compassion, kindness)
2. Capacity to penetrate (go through, break through, pierce)
3. Sensitivity (feeling, warmth, understanding)
4. Separate (disconnect, take apart, divide)
5. Devious (tricky, scheming, underhanded)
6. Take charge (take control, take over, assume responsibility)
7. Seducer (one who leads somebody astray, win somebody over)
8. Indefinite (vague, unclear, indistinct)
9. Initiate (start, kickoff, instigate)

---

[169] Morgan, 269-272.

10. Feeling (having emotions, sentimental, sensitive)
11. Creative (original, inspired, artistic)
12. Receptive (open, interested, friendly)
13. Stands firmly over and against (unmovable, steadfast, determined)
14. Elusive (hard to pin down, indescribable, mysterious)
15. Articulates (communicate something, speak intelligibly, speak distinctly)
16. Jealous (envious, resentful, desirous)
17. Expressive (open, meaningful, significant)
18. Yielding (soft, squashy, compliant)
19. Understanding (considerate, thoughtful, appreciative)
20. What one word or phrase best describes your wife?
21. What word or phrase best describes your wife?

B. Which positions should the pastor's husband hold in the church?

C. When the wife is honored in an anniversary or appreciation service, should the husband also be honored? If so, how?

D. How might your life be different if you, as well as others, knew specifically what your role should entail?

E. Based on a scale of one to ten (1-10), would you change how you are perceived in your present role as the pastor's husband? What number would you choose?

F. Would you like to be recognized as "first gentleman" in the future?

G. List at least three to five tangible things (able to be touched, able to be realized) that describe the role of the pastor's husband.

In summary, the methodology of this project is from a male perspective on the role of the "first husband" or "first gentleman." The data collected will be analyzed and the findings reported in chapter 4, "Project Results and Analysis," and presented in the seminar titled "The Role of the Female Pastor's Husband." The reliability and validity of the research hinge on the respondents' honest responses to the survey and interview questions. The top three skill areas of the men in their role as a pastor's husband will be based on the questions answered by the men. It is anticipated that they will be categorized under leadership, mentorship, and brotherhood. In addition to the studies by Jim Wright and Lillian Daniel, the definitive findings will be discussed in chapter 4 and in the conclusion.

Part II: Implementation of Ethnographic Project and the Plan for Ethical Accountability

Implementation of Project

This chapter section provides an overview of how the project was implemented. The idea of researching the role of the female pastor's husband came to light while I was sitting in the project seminar class at Wesley Theological Seminary in Washington, DC, where Dr. Lewis Parks, dean of the doctoral program, facilitated the course. We had discussed previously my researching the effectiveness of teleconferencing in ministry as the project thesis. During a "round robin" discussion and suggestion session, I felt a sense of urgency to select the topic, "The role of the female pastor's husband." Furthermore, I often thought about the pastor's husband because I sometimes sympathize with my husband as I face the challenges, concerns, and issues of pastorship. In my mind and heart, I would say, "Lord, when we got married, he did not ask to be a pastor's husband, and he has to bear what I sometimes have to bear." Then I would remind myself, "Well, is that not what *for better or for worse* means? Is it not what I had to endure when he was away at the police academy and had to work various hours of night as a state trooper?" So it is with a husband and wife team that God puts together. Your love will endure through the toughest of times with God as your guide. I finally realized that when God prepared and called me for the ministry, He also called and prepared my husband.

Immediately after I selected my research question ("What is the role of the female pastor's husband?"), Dr. Parks suggested that I be more specific and add, "in the House of God Church, Pentecostal Holiness denomination." The participants from my home church serving as the population to be studied would make the research more reliable. Instantly, I began to list the names of married couples I knew where the wife was a pastor. For this ethnographic study, no limitations were placed on the number of years married, nor the length of time the wife pastored.

Next, I met with Bishop Rebecca W. Fletcher, chief overseer of the House of God Church, and State Elder Kenneth Ellis, prelate of District of Columbia, Maryland, Virginia, and California, who gave this project their approval and blessing. Later, a meeting was scheduled to ask the men about their willingness to participate in a study of this kind.

Fifteen couples came to mind, ten of whom I was acquainted with and had the opportunity to observe their interactions with their wives. It was determined that a sample population of ten participants would be selected for the study.

During the 2010 general assembly in Nashville, Tennessee (the House of God headquarters), observations as well as other encounters were recorded in a journal and later documented on the data grid (see appendix 3). This would later assist in analysis of the couples' behavioral patterns. Some of these couples and I serve on the same committees. Two of the husbands report to me, their general elder. In my culture, it is a practice for a woman to respect a married man's wife by first approaching the wife if one desires to engage her husband for advice or to help with a chore, etc. Therefore, the wives were approached for this study. The study was explained to them, along with the level of their husbands' participation in the survey and interview concerning their role as the pastor's husband. Some of the wives were excited and thought it to be an excellent research challenge. Among the fifteen husbands, the project was discussed, with ten willing to participate. Eight of the individuals live in the contiguous United

States, and two live in Jamaica. The ten participants were advised that the study would not pose any risk to them, nor to the church. The confidentiality and anonymity of the participants would be honored. Participants also identified as respondents were assigned a respondent number one through ten. To participate in this project, all were given a cover letter (see appendix 5) and asked to read, sign, and return a consent form that acknowledged their anonymity (see appendix 6). The aforementioned forms, along with the survey and interview questionnaire forms, were mailed to six of the respondents through the United States Postal Service; three were e-mailed, and one was faxed. All of the respondents returned the required forms in a timely manner. However, it was necessary to call two of the respondents as a reminder two weeks ahead of the September 15, 2010, deadline.

The survey and interview questions were distributed to the ten respondents on July 8, 2010. Participants were given a deadline of August 15, 2010, to respond and return the survey questions. They were given an "achievable homework" and were asked to review the interview questions that would be asked of them at a later date. The participants were given the option to type or handwrite on additional paper their responses. A pre-addressed return envelope was provided for each individual's forms mailed, and they were to return the surveys by August 15, 2010. Instructions of the same were given to those emailed and faxed. Follow-up calls were made on July 15, 2010, and telephone interviews were scheduled between August 15 and September 15, 2010. Eight participants had submitted surveys by July 31, 2010, and the other two submitted their forms on August 30 and 31, 2010. Telephone interviews began on August 15 and were completed on August 31, 2010, for three of the respondents. Face-to-face interviews were scheduled at conferences and assemblies for six of the respondents in states where they resided. I had the opportunity to interview one respondent who was in my town on business. Telephone interviews were conducted for the remaining three respondents. The willingness and enthusiasm of the participants made this portion of the study enjoyable.

A Google search was conducted to obtain contact information for authors Dr. Lillian Daniel, Mr. Jim Wright, and Dr. Howard Stone. This did not result in an e-mail response. A face-to-face interview was held in September 2010 with General Elder Jeanette Lott, granddaughter of the late Bishop Janie Lee Ashberry Tate and Reverend Robert Tate, to acquire information concerning the role of a pastor's husband. General Elder Lott shared information about Reverend Robert Tate, husband of the founder, the late Bishop Mary Magdalena Tate, and later of General Elder Lott's grandmother after the founder's death. A telephone interview with Mrs. Irene Montegues, second president of the Second Episcopal District Clergy Family Organization (AME) was successful in that she faxed a copy of the conference newsletter with the "Role of the Male Spouses" workshop conducted by Reverend Glen. Due to unforeseen events, he was unavailable for comments at the time of this writing. Compiling and analyzing the data was the most time-consuming and tedious part of the process.

Counseling Prerequisites

The researcher of any ethnographic study must first be prepared for what may or may not be anticipated in the counseling session. It is inevitable that the works of Edward Wimberly, Pamela Cooper-White, and Robert C. Dykstra are considered in the counseling work to be conducted in this study. Their works were the foundation that influenced me to concentrate on being an effective pastoral counselor. Prior to scheduling an interview or counseling session with the respondents, a review of the authors' literature was conducted. Re-reading the works of the noted theologians/authors was necessary for the success of this study. Wimberly dispels numerous myths that caregivers are confronted with and that make them question their calling. Four areas of concern are discussed: personal issues and encounters with empowerment, marital life issues, family life issues, and challenges of ministry.[170] The researcher must be sure of her life and marital relationship before entering into the counseling session.

---

[170] Edward P. Wimberly, *Recalling Our Own Stories: Spiritual Renewal for Religious Caregivers.* The Jossey-Bass religion-in-practice series. San Francisco: Jossey-Bass Publishers, 1997, xiii.

It was brought to light that many ministers are confronted with the myth of perfection. With that mindset, they neglect to be empathetic with those needing counseling. In addition, one cannot become engulfed with personal issues such as rejection, powerlessness, invulnerability, and self-sacrifice because it will interfere with the ability to be objective and non-judgmental.

Marital and family myths have drastically impacted ministry work in caregivers. Often, family traditions place undue burdens on committed persons. Wimberly warns against allowing negative family myths to dominate because it tends to be portrayed in our role as caregivers.[171] The researcher had to remember that each household is operated differently. No one can say the others are wrong in their methodology: to each his own.

Taking time for self-assessment and reflection of the myths to be rewritten is necessary to understand and help others. It was necessary to re-author[172] my life in order to be objective, unbiased, and compassionate.

Pamela Cooper-White contends that in order for a counseling relationship to be effective, there must be shared wisdom between the counselor or caregiver/helper and the client or one receiving care/helpee. This process of countertransference[173] must take place to elicit a positive exchange of energy. In order to effectively counsel someone, the counselor must first recognize his or her own "unresolved issues."[174] Entering the counseling session, the researcher was confident of self and was open to hear what the participants had to say.

The researcher reflected on the book *Images of Pastoral Care,* which introduces the reader to some of the works of Anton T. Boisen.[175] Through the works of Boisen's personal experiences, he strove to introduce clergy and seminary students to the ministry of psychiatric patients in the hospital. Through his research, he determined that

---

[171]   Wimberly, *Recalling,* 51.
[172]   Wimberly, *Recalling,* 125.
[173]   Cooper-White, vii.
[174]   Ibid.
[175]   Dykstra, 161.

every patient had the potential of being a "living human document"[176] and to be examined psychologically. According to Dykstra, Charles V. Gerkin contended that pastoral counselors are valued for more than just being listeners, but they too have a relational story to share.[177] Bonnie McLemore recognized a human web beyond male counselors and introduced a feminist side of psychological counseling.[178] As a woman pastor having to counsel male congregants, the researcher concurs with McLemore. A counselor must be well-rounded and capable of uncovering untruths that may interfere with healing and revealing truths. Paul W. Pruyser views the counselor as a clinical psychologist or "diagnostician."[179] It is, therefore, necessary to consider the varied personalities of the husbands and to utilize the most effective approach when interviewing. During the interview process with the respondents, as a pastoral counselor, I individually approached each participant with an open mind. It was imperative that I remain nonjudgmental during the interview and throughout the study in order to have a reliable and valid study.

Plan for Ethical Accountability

Honesty with the participants is of utmost importance. Participants were provided a consent form, which was reviewed with them to explain and disclose facts about confidentiality and anonymity. Signatures from the participant and researcher validate consent to conduct the interview. Pseudonyms or a numerical coding system will be used. In this study, the participants were identified as respondents one to ten.

Data will be stored electronically on a USB flash drive which is password protected. Hard copies and journal entries from interviews will be locked in a storage bin and maintained for three years, except in the event that materials are needed for further research (for

---

[176] Cooper-White, 22-29.
[177] Dykstra, 30.
[178] Dykstra, 44.
[179] Dykstra, 161.

example, writing of a book). In order to provide ethical accountability, I prepared an application for the Institutional Review Board (see appendix 7).

Part III: History of the House of God Church

Historical Background of the House of God Church, Founder, and Co-Laborers

This section includes a historical background of the House of God Church's founder, Mary Magdalena Lewis Tate; her sons, Walter Curtis Lewis and Felix Early Lewis; her co-laborers; and a brief account of the modern-day House of God Church and its doctrinal beliefs. An overview of the relational patterns of male and female pastors and their spouses within the House of God Church is also discussed.

This project was approached prayerfully and with the blessings of my senior administrator, Bishop Rebecca W. Fletcher, chief overseer and fifth administrator of the House of God, which is the Church of the Living God, the Pillar and Ground of the Truth without Controversy, Inc. Keith Dominion. This body, which belongs to the Pentecostal denomination, provides my spiritual covering on earth. The name of the church, although it is quite long, was adopted by the founder from Scripture (1 Timothy 3:15-16a, KJV), which reads, "But if I tarry long, that thou mayest know how thou oughtest to behave thyself in the house of God, which is the church of the living God, the pillar and ground of the truth. And without controversy great is the mystery of godliness."

The church was established in 1903 by an African American female named Mary Magdalena Lewis Tate (1871-1930), who named the visible church on earth after what she believed and taught as the name of the invisible church of all baptized believers for eternity.[180] She taught that the invisible church is the waiting and prepared bride

---

[180] *The Constitution Government and General Decree of the Church of the Living God, the Pillar and Ground of the Truth, Inc.* Nashville, TN: The New and Living Way Publishing Co., 1989 Reprint.

of Christ, according to Scriptures[181]Revelation 21:2. Bishop Meharry Lewis describes Bishop Tate as being the first female bishop and chief overseer during the Holiness Movement in the United States; she was reared in the Methodist tradition.[182] Bishop Tate's disciplines were inclusive of teaching "equality in the sexes in the sight of God"[183] and that "holiness is a way of life."[184]

Bishop Lewis further paints a portrait of Bishop Tate's husband and the role he played in the church. Her husband, Robert Tate, was a deacon in the church. He demonstrated leadership, mentorship, and brotherhood characteristics as the bishop's spouse. His role included an active engagement in guiding and encouraging new converts and coordinating meetings/services for individuals to hear Bishop Tate evangelize, teach, preach, and heal. As the pastor's husband, Deacon Tate motivated individuals to be involved in church activities. Bishop Tate would lead individuals to Christ, and Deacon Tate would assist with retaining their membership.[185]

In an interview with General Elder Jeanette Lott of the House of God Church, she confirms the works of Deacon Tate after the passing of Mother Tate, founder. Deacon Tate later became Reverend Tate and married her grandmother, Bishop Janie Lee Ashberry Tate, presiding bishop of the House of God in Detroit, Michigan, in the 1950s. Both Bishop Janie Lee Tate and Reverend Tate worked as a team, setting up missions and leading individuals to Christ. They continued in the same vein of evangelism as described by Bishop Lewis.

The House of God Church continues its stance in defending women's leadership through the teachings of its overseers, bishops, elders, ministers, deacons, members, and youth. The second chief

---

181   Constitution and Government, 33.

182   Meharry Lewis. *Mary Lena Lewis Tate: "A Street Called Straight" (Acts 9:11): The Ten Most Dynamic and Productive Black Female Holiness Preachers of the Twentieth Century.* The New and Living Way Publishing Company, Nashville, TN: 2002, 14.

183   Lewis, 13.

184   Lewis, 19.

185   Lewis, 11.

overseer, Bishop Mary F. L. Keith, wrote an article, *Shall Women Lead, Preach, or Preside Over the Flock of God?* Bishop Keith responds to this question by saying, "The answer to this question is a dynamic *yes* with biblical proof. God has made no distinction in His kingdom between men and women: they all have the same happy privileges."[186] Bishop Keith supports this with Scriptures from the word of God by recognizing the call to Zipporah, Miriam, Deborah, Hannah, Huldah, and of course, the great works of Mother Mary L. Tate, the visible founder and first chief overseer of our church.

Historical documentation from *The Constitution, Government and General Decree of the Church of the Living God, the Pillar and Ground of the Truth, Inc.* states that Mother Tate was moved by God, the Holy Spirit, to preach the Gospel to the world. She first acknowledged her call to the ministry in Steel Springs, Tennessee.[187] Lewis contends that the absence of her husband's acceptance of her call to ministry ultimately led to their separation.[188] She moved to Paducah, Kentucky, and took her two young sons, Walter Curtis Lewis and Felix Early Lewis, whom she chose as her co-laborers. Mother Tate's call and commission to the ministry were revealed assuredly in Paducah. With limited finances and in obedience to God, Mother Tate left her sons in the care of her sisters in Paducah so that she could venture on her assigned missionary journey.

The House of God archives record that she sailed from Paducah, Kentucky, to Brooklyn, Illinois, on the Ohio River as her sons watched with tearful eyes.[189] Her first sermon preached in Brooklyn, Illinois, was with power and the anointing of God. Individuals of all age groups were moved by the Holy Spirit as she preached the Word of

---

[186] Mary F. L. Keith, "Female Leadership Defended." *The Holy Bible* (KJV). Specifically designed for the House of God Church, Inc. Nashville, TN: Publishers, Inc., before 1962, reprint 1971.

[187] Constitution and Government, 4.

[188] Meharry H. Lewis. *Mary Lena Lewis Tate: "A Street Called Straight" (Acts 9:11): The Ten Most Dynamic and Productive Black Female Holiness Preachers of the Twentieth Century.* Nashville, TN: The New and Living Way Publishing Company, 2002, 5-6.

[189] *Constitution Government,* 4.

God in cleanliness (sanctification). When she was able to provide for her sons, she retrieved them from her sisters, and the family traveled to Paris, Tennessee. Bishop Tate preached as her sons bowed in prayer on the streets of Paris. The power of her anointing when she preached the Word of God authenticated her "apostleship and bishopric to which God had foreordained her."[190] She preached in the homes of people of various colors and creeds. Men and women were overjoyed in the spirit by the word preached. She was styled by various ethnic groups as "a great Eastern traveler."[191] On her missionary journey of preaching the Gospel in the state of Alabama, "over nine hundred people repented and were converted and turned to Christ."[192]

As Bishop Tate traveled the southern states, she established bands or missions in various locations. In 1908, she became ill, was pronounced uncurable, and was bedridden. While she was on her bed of affliction, God's glory fell on and in her. She received the baptism of the Holy Ghost, with the Bible evidence of speaking in other and unknown tongues as the Spirit of God gave utterance, as on the Day of Pentecost in Acts, chapter 2.[193] God healed and sealed Mother Tate as she leaped from her bed and began to go out to preach and teach others the "good news" of the Holy Ghost's Gospel. Later in 1908, the first general assembly was held in Greenville, Alabama, where preachers from all the churches established were ordained and pastors were appointed. She was also ordained in this general assembly as chief overseer of the church and served until her death.[194]

Mother Tate taught love, peace, and equality; yet, she encountered sexism within her own ranks. Mother Tate sent certain male officials to set up works in the House of God Church's name; however, they absconded with funds the church gave them, split from the HOGC, and established their own organizations while at the same time

---

[190] Ibid.

[191] Ibid.

[192] Ibid.

[193] *Constitution Government*, 6.

[194] *Constitution Government*, 6-7.

infringing upon a part of the church's name.[195] In spite of efforts by those opposed to women's leadership, the church spread to over twenty states in the United States and abroad. By 1911 and 1914, the church had its first Constitution and General Decree printed in book form.

The death of Bishop Mary Magdalena Lewis Tate in 1930 weighed heavily on the church, and division among some people increased over who would be the next chief overseer. Although Bishop Mary F. Lewis Keith served as chief overseer of the entire body for a while, a court ruling in the Chancery Court, Part One, at Nashville, Tennessee, on October 27, 1938, recommended the decision of just one chief overseer of all the people. In overturning the decision, they agreed to uphold the May 1931 decision of the supreme executive council of the House of God Church, which stated, "Due to the times of change of conditions, and due to the present condition and spirit of the people, that three competent persons be appointed and ordained to fill the office of chief overseer and that accordingly, Bishop Felix E. Lewis, Bishop Mary F. Keith, and Bishop Bruce L. McLeod were elected as chief overseers to preside over sixteen states each."[196] Today, there are three dominions: Keith Dominion, Lewis Dominion, and Jewell (previously McLeod) Dominion. My membership is with the Keith Dominion.

Description of the Modern-Day House of God Church

The chief overseer/senior bishop's office is perpetual, and upon his/her death, lots are cast to select a new overseer (patterned after the apostles' practice in Acts 1:23-26), after fasting and praying for three days and nights. The overseer is then ordained by the quorum of chief helpers, bishops, and elders of the dioceses that are a part of the selection process.[197]

Since the death of Bishop Tate, the first chief overseer, there have been four chief overseers (two males and two females): Bishop Mary

---

[195] *Constitution Government,* 93.

[196] Ibid.

[197] *Constitution Government,* 78-79.

F. Lewis Keith, second chief overseer; Bishop James W. Jenkins, third chief overseer; Bishop James C. Elliott, fourth chief overseer; and Bishop Rebecca W. Fletcher, DD, of Pine Hill, New Jersey, who is the current and fifth chief overseer. Since its inception, the House of God has been an egalitarian system (rule is by male and/or female). We believe that whom God calls, He qualifies.

The church's history, constitution, and government, hierarchal leadership structure, doctrinal stance, relationship between pastors and spouses, and differences in male and female leadership styles have existed since its inception. The chief overseer is president of the incorporation; she is also the senior bishop, general moderator, senior editor, and apostle elder of the church.

A rule book is needed in any government to serve as a guide, as are the Holy Scriptures for mankind. The Constitution Government and General Decree of the Church of the Living God, the Pillar and Ground of the Truth is 112 pages long, containing the rules, laws, faith and doctrine, sacraments, procedures, etc. of the church.

The church is hierarchal in administration, with an "official organ" consisting of the senior bishop or chief overseer, chief helpers, quorum of bishops, state elders, general elders, presiding elders, elders (ordained and trial), ministers (ordained and local), exhorters (those who have acknowledged their call to ministry and are still in the school of experience), and deacons (ordained and trial). There are three levels in the church: local, state, and general. This follows the "Jethro Principle" (Exodus 18:14-27) and also introduces delegation of authority and leadership accountability. General is the highest level. All three levels are subject to the chief overseer and general assembly (representatives of the entire organization). In the church, I presently serve as a general elder (ordained) presiding over four churches on the general level, as state preparation chairperson on the state level in Maryland, and as pastor at my home church on the local level. The highest governing board is the supreme executive council, composed of twelve bishops and state elders in addition to alternates (which may consist of bishops, elders, and ordained deacons). The second-highest governing board is the general trustee board, composed of twelve bishops and state elders with alternates (which may consist of bishops, elders, and ordained deacons).

Individuals are appointed by the chief overseer/senior bishop of the church and endorsed by the general assembly (entire church community) to serve in appointed positions as pastors, elders, presiding elders, general elders, state elders, and bishops after they successfully pass each stage and criteria for success. Chief helpers are also appointed by the chief overseer to assist the chief overseer. Bishops and state elders are appointed to supervise a state or district. General elders are appointed to be a liaison to the bishop or state elder and chief overseer.

The church's doctrinal beliefs and teachings are based on the foundation of the Holy Scriptures. The following are some beliefs that are taught:

> We believe and really know according to the word of Christ, that it is necessary to observe and keep the commandment of Christ by washing one another's feet as was His example to do as He did;
>
> We believe it is right and necessary to observe the Lord's Supper or Passover as He did with His disciples before He was crucified by using unleavened bread as a token of His body and by using pure unadulterated water as a token and agreement of His blood, as nothing except water will agree with His blood. (St. John 19:34)
>
> Read on this subject the following Scriptures: Wine forbidden by the word of God (Leviticus 10-8-10; Hosea 4-11; Hosea 9:4; Luke 1:15; and Mark 15:23); Water approved of by the word of God: (1 Corinthians 10:1: 4; Exodus 17:6; Matthew 10:42; Mark 9:41; and Revelation 22:16-17);
>
> We believe in praying; We believe in fasting; We believe in keeping the Sabbath with the covenant which is God, Christ and the Holy Ghost, instead of with types and shadows which was fulfilled by *the* coming of Christ; We believe that to cease from our own works is to cease from sin;
>
> We believe that Christ hath given us rest from sin, evil and confusion in our bodies instead of rest from carnal

labor which is necessary for the sustenance of our temporal bodies; We believe there is a place of inheritance and joy and happiness beyond expression for those that long for the appearing of the Lord, to those that keep His sayings and do His will; and that this place is not a place of carnal rest, for they rest neither day nor night there, but continually give glory to God; We believe that eyes have not seen, neither have ears heard, what is in store in that city for those that love the Lord, do His will and keep His commandments; We believe that flesh and blood cannot enter there, that sorrow and sighing are not there and that nothing that sin or worketh iniquity, nor any sin has ever been or can ever enter there. This place we believe is eternal into Heaven and is the Heaven of heavens.

We believe that there is a final Judgment Day in store for all, both the good and for the bad. In it we believe that sinners will be justly judged, condemned and separated from the righteous and turned into the place called the Lake of Fire and Brimstone, prepared for those that do evil for the wicked and for the devil and his angels.[198]

We believe in God the Father, God the Son, and God the Holy Ghost, and that these three are one in holy estate of power of the God-head.

We believe God the Father, God the Son, and God the Holy Ghost are three powers of the holy union of heaven, being expressly called us! (Genesis 1:26) We preach and do firmly believe that Jesus Christ is the Son of the Living God, and that He was born of the Virgin Mary, that He was spiritually conceived and brought forth of the Virgin Mary thus taking upon Himself the likeness of sinful flesh and for sin condemned sin in the flesh; that the righteousness of the law might be fulfilled in us, who walk not after the flesh, but after the Spirit. By which He was conceived in the Virgin Mary and brought forth in the likeness of every man in order to convince man of the very fact that human flesh can live in this world free from sin and condemnation (Romans 8th chapter).

---

[198] Constitution and Government, 32

We believe and do firmly preach that Jesus Christ is the way and our example giver was baptized or filled with the Holy Ghost and thereby was made able to resist the temptations of the devil (read Matthew 3.16 and 4:1 to 11;" 'That He spake with unknown tongues' (read Matthew 27:46; Mark 15:34;" We believe that all Christian followers must be filled with the same spirit in order to be able to resist the temptations of the devil and to overcome the world, and to live free from sin in this world (read Matthew 3:11; Mark 1:8; Luke 3:16; St. John 1:33-34; St. John 8:34-36; Titus 2:11-14."[199]

We believe and do firmly preach that the gospel of Jesus Christ is the power of God unto salvation, unto every one that believeth it, and that the gospel do remit sins, and that the gospel began in and with the apostles at Jerusalem by the Holy Ghost that was given unto them, and that the Holy Ghost is the power of God and is the Gospel (Romans 1:16; Luke 24:46-49; Acts 1:5-8; and Acts 2:1: 4;"

We believe and do firmly preach the Bible evidence of receiving the baptism of the Holy Ghost and fire is speaking with tongues as the Spirit of God giveth utterance, as on the day of Pentecost as mentioned in Acts 2:1 to 4; and that the tongues spoken in and through the utterance given by the spirit, may not be understood by man and may be unknown to men, but is understood of God (read I Corinthians 14:2); and that the unknown tongue is a sign of God's victory over sin and the wicked purposes of vain men and their wicked imaginations (read Genesis 11:1 to 6); and that the unknown and divers tongues have always served to frustrate and stop the sinful purposes and attempts of wicked men and to establish the purpose and will of God (read Genesis 11:7 to 9);"[200]

"Wherefore tongues are for a sign not to them that believe but to them that believe not (read I Corinthians 14:22); We believe and firmly preach that people are justified and made clean through faith and by the words of Christ

---

[199] *Constitution Government*, 63-64.
[200] *Constitution Government*, 64.

(read St. John 15:3); and that we are glorified and made wholly sanctified by receiving the baptism of the Holy Ghost and fire with Bible evidence;

We believe that there are two stages of sanctification: First your sanctification (read I Thessalonians 4.3); and Secondly, wholly sanctification which is also glorification of the body through the spirit of the living God (read I Thessalonians 4:4); We believe that Jesus Christ died to save His People from sin and that His blood cleanseth us from all sin (read I John 1:7-10); We believe that Jesus is the foundation of the Church, and that such a foundation was finished when He said on the cross it is finished (read St. John 19:30 and Paul's quotation in Ephesians 2:19 to 22);"

"We believe that God created man, male and female, man in His own image and likeness and that man being in the image and likeness of God was perfect, pure, and holy and free from all sin so long as He remained and abided in the image and likeness of God (read Genesis 1:27; I John 3:1 to 5); and that for the experience of sin, and appreciation of righteousness, man was permitted to be his own moral agent of decision and acceptations of life through righteousness of death through sin and disobedience. He disobeyed, transgressed, sinned and died. We believe through the fall of Adam from righteousness into sin through disobedience that death reigned for a time over all men even unto all (read Romans 5:12 to 21);

We believe that through the disobedience of one man many were made sinners and that through the obedience of one, even Christ, many shall be made righteous and that in and through Christ we have access again to the tree of life to live again in the image and likeness of God. Perfect, pure and free from sin with the purposed experience and worry of sin and finally with the acceptance and high appreciation of salvation from sin through Christ the Lord from heaven and the tree of life. Amen."[201]

Although our doctrinal beliefs are extensive, they are inclusive of what the engrafted Word of God commands us to believe and

---

[201] Ibid.

obey. We also observe ordinances and sacraments commended in the Word of God.

There are nine sacraments observed by the HOGC: baptism of the Holy Ghost, baptism of repentance, baptism of water, Eucharist, foot washing, unction, holy matrimony, ordination, and confirmation. The church holds to the tradition of "winning souls to Christ" (the Great Commission) as a priority, and it is reflected in the order of service. Service begins with the call to worship by one of the ministers, who also conducts the service. The devotional service begins with two deacons, who begin with a spiritual song. A second spiritual song is sung, which is followed by a metered hymn. One deacon leads the metered hymn, while the second deacon leads the prayer. The selected metered hymn is intended to prime the hearts of anyone who desires to be "touched" by the Lord. An invitation is given to the congregation to testify or "story-weave."[202] Sharing the testimonies always encourages those needing an uplift. The order of service changes after the devotional period: announcements are given, and a welcome to visitors is extended. Next, the trustees receive tithes and offerings from the congregants. This is followed by a Scripture reading and selection by a choir. Poetry is sometimes presented, or a congregational song, after which the speaker for the day is presented to the congregation. Another selection is provided by the congregation, followed by the preacher or God's messenger for the day. Normally, with the exception of Youth Sunday, the pastor preaches. On Youth Sunday, the trained youth carry out the service and will sometimes present a youth speaker. After the Gospel message, a spiritual song of hope is sung. The altar call that includes an invitation to discipleship and the opening of the doors of the church are offered. A prayer is offered, and the anointing of oil for healing, upon special request, is administered. Individuals may also have a special testimony of God's miraculous blessing of deliverance after the altar call. The service concludes with closing remarks and the benediction.

Music in the church is lively. The House of God is renowned for introducing "sacred steel" (steel guitar) to the church community.

---

[202] Anderson and Foley, xiii.

Other musical instruments offered up in praise to God include the drums, electric guitar, bass guitar, keyboard, organ, saxophone, and tambourines. The church believes in preaching, praying, singing, and praising God with a shout, known as a "holy dance."

The ethnicity of the church at large is comprised of ninety-five percent African American and the other five percent is mixed multi-culturally. Efforts to diversify membership through church growth are done by reaching out to the un-churched and culturally diverse, as mandated when carrying out the universal church vision: " . . . to lead men and women out of sin and degradation into the light and uplift of Christ and to the kingdom of God."[203] Discrimination on the basis of gender, race, class, or age is not condoned in the church.[204] Equality for all is encouraged, and individuals are recognized for their God-given talents and works. Those aspiring to the bishopric must successfully pass the stages preceding, beginning with the exhorter level.[205] The membership consists of various professionals: doctors and other medical professionals, attorneys, counselors, psychiatrists, teachers, accountants, retirees, youth workers, and other white- and blue-collar workers.

There are 167 churches incorporated in this body, of which 50% (83) are guided by female pastors and 50% (84) have male pastors[206] (table 3.1, appendix 8). There are 24 dioceses or districts that encompass the 167 churches; there are a total of 14 bishops and 1 state elder who serve as prelates/bishops of these dioceses (table 3.2, appendix 9).

Description of Male and Female Pastors and Their Spouses within the House of God Church

Based on observations of the pastors and spouses in the House of God church, the pastors and spouses demonstrate the love, respect, unity,

---

[203] *Constitution Government,* 3.

[204] *Constitution Government,* 58.

[205] *Constitution Government,* 35.

[206] House of God Statistical Church Report 2010, Nashville, TN.

and support they have for one another. The couples are inseparable: when you see one, the other is right there. They jointly serve on most committees and appear together at various functions. During sickness, each is with his or her spouse to care for and nurture him or her back to health. These couples exhibit great faith and share a viable prayer life. They are always well groomed and have a genuine concern for others. They are givers of themselves and their finances, and they always have an outstretched hand to help others. The unity these couples openly demonstrate often shields differences in male pastor and female pastor leadership styles. In most cases, if the pastor is a male, his spouse conducts his administrative affairs. However, if the pastor is a female, she engages the services of another female to conduct her administrative affairs, if she does not carry them out herself. Usually, the female pastor will obtain the services of a family member.

From personal experience, my husband is confident and a man of integrity. He is sure of himself and is not threatened by the pastor's position in the church. These characteristics were also observed among the female pastors' husbands interviewed in the study. These husbands are men of compassion and possess the full nature of God within: possessing both male and female attributes, as does God. This makes them one in Christ with their spouses.

Deacon Jarris L. Taylor, Sr. and some of the other husbands have publically acknowledged that God has chosen, called, and commissioned certain women to serve as leaders of His people, including their spouses. The bottom line is that female pastors and their spouses are truly helpers one with another (Ephesians 2:10). If the husband truly loves his wife as he loves himself in Christ, there is no room for envy nor strife, but unity and peace in Christ Jesus: "Husbands, love your wives, even as Christ also loved the church, and gave himself for it" (Ephesians 5:25).

Chapter 4

Project Results and Analysis

Survey Results of Respondents

This study is based on the findings of ten husbands (known as respondents) out of the fifteen contacted. Surveys were initially given to the husbands to collect demographic information and answer basic questions. Interviews followed the surveys and had more specific questions to compare commonalities. The respondents in this study will define their own role as the husbands of female pastors, just as the males of the Second District Council of African Methodist Episcopalians in Baltimore, Maryland, did recently (refer to chapter 3, part II). The respondents will have ownership of their role in the church because they were proactive in developing these guidelines. The survey form consisted of two parts. Part I identified demographics of the respondents. They were the first nine questions. Part II contained six survey questions. Results of the survey questions are presented from the actual responses of the ten respondents, as following:

Demographics: Questions 1-9

- Question 1 addressed the ages of the respondents. One respondent (10%) is between the ages of 41 and 50 years old; one respondent (10%) is between the ages of 51 and 60 years old; six respondents (60%) are between the ages of 61 and 70 years old; and two respondents (20%) are over the age of 71 years old (table 4.1).

- Question 2 identified the ethnicity of the respondents. Eight of the respondents (80%) are African American; one respondent (10%) is of African descent, and one respondent (10%) of Jamaican descent (table 4.2).

- Question 3 addresses the respondents' religious denomination prior to marriage to the pastor. One respondent had no religious affiliation (10%); one respondent was with Church of God in Christ Holiness (10%); one respondent was previously in an Apostolic Holiness Church (10%); and seven respondents (70%) were born and reared in the House of God Church (table 4.3).

- Question 4 inquired as to the number of years the respondents were married and the wife a pastor. Four respondents (40%) were married less than ten years while their wives served as pastor; 30% (three) respondents were married less than twenty years while their wives served as pastor; and 30% (three) respondents were married up to thirty years while their wives served as pastor (table 4.4).

- Question 5 asked if their wives pastored before they were married. Only one respondent (10%) married his wife when she was already a pastor. Therefore, nine respondents (90%) married before the wife was appointed to pastor a church (table 4.5).

- Question 6 reveals the number of years the couples have been married. Three respondents (30%) have been married less than twenty years; three respondents (30%) have been married between thirty-one and thirty-nine years; two respondents (20%) have been married between forty-five and forty-seven years; and two respondents (20%) have been married fifty years and over (table 4.6).

- Question 7 asked if they had been previously married. Only two of the ten respondents (20%) have been married previously. The other eight (80%) have been married once (table 4.7).

- Question 8 inquired if the couple had school-age children. Two of the ten (20%) have school-age children; therefore, the other eight (80%) do not (table 4.8).
- Question 9 asked the respondent's occupation. The majority of the husbands are "blue-collar workers." The occupations range from ministers to security officers. Four are retirees but continue to work; two are educators; one is a maintenance manager; one is a church musician; one is a professional truck driver; and one is a waiter and security officer (table 4.9).

Survey: Questions 10-15

- Question 10 asks, "How would you describe your role as the pastor's husband?" The various responses include "chauffeur for wife and church members"; "joint decision-maker as co-pastors"; "work as a team member"; "scheduler of wife's meetings"; "provider of moral and spiritual support"; and "serve in the capacity of deacon, mediator, trustee, subtle warrior (keeping things in order), helper, and mission worker."
- Question 11 asked, "What are your wife's expectations of you in the church?" The responses were as follows: as a co-pastor, to conduct ecclesiastical and administrative functions, visitations, teach, preach and evangelize; as a deacon and member, to be an example; to lead; to respect; to be dedicated to God and wife; to be on time, to participate in most church activities; to maintain high standards; to support wife in whatever vision God gives her for the church; and to help maintain church order.
- Question 12 asked, "What are the members' expectations of you as pastor's husband?" The responses were as follows: to work with wife as a team member; to demonstrate exemplary leadership; to participate in church activities; to support the efforts of the pastor and personally care for her (administratively, spiritually, and as a husband);

to offer support on all levels; to be an armor bearer; and to attend appointments with wife.

- Question 13 asked, "What do you like best about being the pastor's husband?" One respondent said that it keeps him on his toes and alert. Others mentioned traveling and meeting different people, and two respondents said, "Sitting at the head table at dinner functions."
- Question 14 asked, "What do you like least about being the pastor's husband?" The respondents' responses were as follows: roles may become confusing and cause marital conflicts, reprimands from the wife; sharing wife's time with others; pressure and hard work upon wife; his need to be saved; people expecting more from him; having to adjust his personal schedule to accommodate the pastor; sharing one half of the finances if co-pastoring; and frequent travel.
- Question 15 asked, "What further training or experience do you think is needed to better prepare you in the role of the pastor's husband?" The responses are as follows: just to have a closer walk with the Lord and the Holy Ghost; formal seminary training; more information on the role of the pastor's husband; how to be a better support to wife; know more of the Bible and church decree; patience; and a training seminar on the expectations of the husbands.

Interview Results of Respondents

- Question 1: "What other positions do you hold in the church presently?" Responses: general elder; co-pastor; trustee; deacon; superintendent of Sunday school; Sunday school teacher; musician; deacon board chairman; deacon board assistant chairman; Young Folks and Friends Union president; Men's Auxiliary president; presiding elder; church administrator; treasurer; usher; and church security officer. One respondent stated he holds no positions.

- Question 2: "What programs have you instituted in the church in your role as pastor's husband?" Responses: organized a men's club; local missionary department; noonday prayer; pastor's aide; and building fund. One respondent said he had not instituted any programs in the church.

- Question 3: "How do you differentiate your roles as pastor's husband, husband and member?" Responses: all of the respondents unanimously agreed that their wives respect them as the head of the house at home; and at church, they respect their wives as the heads over them in the Lord.

- Question 4: "Have you mentored (counseled or given advice to) anyone in the church?" Responses: eight of the respondents said yes, and two said no.

- Question 5: "What is your theological belief concerning female pastors and bishops? What Scriptures may come to mind to support your belief?" Responses: all of the respondents agree that God calls male and female alike to preach His word. Scriptures to support their beliefs are Matthew 28:19-20, Luke chapter 24, and Joel 2:28. Three of the respondents mentioned Galatians 3:28, and one could not provide a Scripture.

- Question 6: "What is your perception of the role of the pastor's husband presently?" Responses: they all agreed that it is an important position because it reflects their love and support for their wives. It is an honorable position. The overall attitude was to be supportive; be active as a leader; to counsel; and to give advice. They also agreed that at home, one must listen to the wife because she has to bear a lot of burdens. One respondent said he did not know what perception people had of him.

- Question 7: "Are there barriers in being a first husband? If so, explain what they are." Responses: one respondent stated he has to avoid trying to run the church and take control from the pastor; sharing the pastor's attention with other male members; people will sometimes shy away from the husband; late-night phone calls; not being filled with the Holy Ghost; and the husband must lead by a good example. One respondent said conflict sometimes comes when the wife fails to concede that the husband is the head of the home: "Conflict in the home will also lead to conflict in the church." Only one respondent said that he sees no barriers.

- Question 8: "Have you discussed the role of the first husband with other first husbands in other denominations? If so, how did they describe their role?" Responses: all responded, "No."

- Question 9: "Have you discussed the role of the first husband with other first husbands within the House of God Church? If so, how did they describe their role?" Responses: nine of the respondents said no. One said yes. He was informed that they are to provide support to their spouses.

- Question 10: "How would you define the role of the pastor's husband for future considerations?" Responses were extensive and inclusive of the following:

  - To provide moral support and spiritual help and be a loving husband at all times.
  - To serve as chauffeur for wife and church members.
  - To help make joint decisions as co-pastors.
  - To work as a team.
  - To help schedule her meetings.
  - To serve as deacon.
  - To be a mediator.
  - To serve as a trustee.
  - To share his experience and expertise with his wife when necessary.
  - To be an armor bearer.
  - To be a helper.
  - To serve as a mission worker.
  - To have self-confidence.

- To have a good relationship with the wife.
- To be reverenced by the wife.
- To be godly, loving, humble.
- To communicate with others.
- To be available when the wife needs him.
- To protect her from physical harm.
- To offer constructive suggestions to better the ministry.
- To relieve her of stressful situations when possible.
- To seek future theological training.
- To seek training in time management.
- To be obedient and first in following the pastor's lead.
- To be an example before the members.
- To follow close behind the deacon chairman.
- To take a leadership role
- To have members follow the positive example of the pastor's husband and everyone will fall in line.
- To live an exemplary life so that other people will not stumble.
- To motivate the members.
- To give financially to the church.
- To lead out.

Responses to Additional Questions

Only five of the ten respondents willingly answered the additional questions. Therefore, five respondents will have no response.

- Question A: "Which of the following nineteen characteristics describe your wife? Check all that apply."

Edward Morgan identifies a combination of masculine and feminine qualities that makes one a more successful leader.[207] Masculine qualities are as follows: capacity to penetrate, separate, take charge, initiate,

---

[207] Edward Morgan, "Implications of the Masculine and the Feminine in Pastoral Ministry."

create, and stand firmly over and against, to articulate and express meaning. Feminine qualities are as follows: tenderness, sensitivity, deviousness, seduction, indefiniteness, feeling, receptivity, elusiveness, jealousy, creative containing, yielding and understanding.

> Distribution of male and female leadership traits of wives according to the husbands' assessments are as follows (table 4.10):
>
> Respondent #1: wife possesses six male traits and four female traits.
>
> Respondent #2: wife possesses six male traits and five female traits.
>
> Respondent #3: wife possesses seven male traits and four female traits.
>
> Respondent #5: wife possesses seven male traits and six female traits.
>
> Respondent #10: wife possesses five male traits and six female traits.

Question: "What one word or phrase best describes your wife?"
Responses:
Respondent #1: Aggressive;
Respondent #2: Straightforward, tells it like it is, does not sugar-coat her words;
Respondent #3: Prayerful:
Respondent #5: Spiritually anointed, firm but fair.
Respondent #10: Persistent.

Journal of Pastoral Care 34 no. 4 (Dec 1980): 268: 277.
-http://newfirstsearch.oclc.org/WebZ/FTFETCH?sessionid=fsapp6-51254-gb2iiz2q-fbvlk7:entitypagenum=243:0:rule=100:fetchtype=fulltext: dbname =ATLA FT:recno=12:resultset=10:ftformat=PDF:format=BI:isbillable =TRUE:numrecs=1:isdirectarticle=FALSE:entityemailfullrecno=12:entityemailfullresultset=10:entityemailftfrom=ATLA FT: [accessed June 30, 2010]

- Question B: "Which positions should the pastor's husband hold in the church?" Responses: Three respondents said the husband should hold whatever position the pastor appoints him to. One said as deacon board or trustee board chairman or minister of music. One said it does not make a difference as long as the man is God-fearing and follows the rules and regulations of the church.

- Question C: "When the wife is honored in an anniversary or appreciation service, should the husband also be honored? If so, how?" Responses: Three respondents said, yes, by verbal recognition and gifts. The men feel that they suffer together; when one hurts, the other hurts. Another said that he gives to her financially in the home and should not provide for her also in the church He feels he should be exempt from giving her pastoral gifts. He holds her up, wipes away her tears, and takes her up and down the road. Of the remaining two, one said, "No, it is the wife's day." He is her helpmeet and sits beside her. Husbands should not exalt themselves. The fifth husband said it is up to the church membership.

- Question D: "How might your life be different if you, as well as others, knew specifically what your role should entail?" Responses: two respondents said it would be better. Two respondents said it would not be any different. One respondent said he would be able to tackle problems with assurance and confidence as a genuine leader and he would be more active.

- Question E: "Based on a scale of one to ten (1-10), would you change how you are perceived in your present role as the pastor's husband? What number would you choose?" Responses: None of the husbands desired to answer this question. They just were not prepared to answer.

- Question F: "Would you like to be recognized as a first husband ('first gentleman') in the future?" Responses: all of the husbands responded, "Yes," with the exception of one, who said he prefers to remain being recognized as the pastor's husband. He feels the pastor should get all the honor for the hard work she does.

- Question G: "List at least three to five tangible things (able to be touched, able to be realized) that describe the role of the pastor's husband." Responses: to be obedient to the Word of God; to be hospitable and show respect to others as any other Christian; to be available for wife; coordinate travel and meetings for wife; usher; serve as church treasurer; clean church; cook food to feed the kids after Sunday school; and church musician.

Analysis of Findings of Study

The survey results of this ethnographic study identify the ten husbands' ages as forty-one years and older. The majority of men are African American, with one being of African descent and another of Jamaican descent. The men, with the exception of one, had a religious upbringing. One husband was from the Apostolic Church, Apostolic faith; one from the Church of God in Christ (COGIC), Pentecostal faith; and eight of the men were born and reared in the House of God Church, Pentecostal faith. It is apparent that most of the men in this study reared in the HOGC married within their own covering.

Evidently, the nine husbands have no issues with women being in leadership positions because they have remained faithful in their marital relationships even after their spouses began their pastoralship. Only one respondent married when his wife was already a pastor; evidently, he knew what he was getting into from the beginning. The range of marital bliss, for seven of the husbands, is from thirty-one years to over fifty years. Three of the respondents have been married less than twenty years. Two of the ten respondents have been married previously, and two other respondents have school-age children.

The occupations of the husbands vary and include two full-time ministers, three retirees, two educators, one bus driver, one musician, and one security officer and part-time waiter. This indicates that these men value providing for their families by being gainfully employed.

When asked how they perceive their present roles as pastors' husbands, their responses demonstrated their love and care for their wives. The husbands support their wives by chauffeuring their wives and members. Providing moral and spiritual support was their main focus. Their roles as husbands in the church included positions of leadership such as deacons, trustees, and musicians. The husbands expressed the fact that their wives expected them to set an example, to be leaders, respectful, active in church affairs, and dedicated to God and their wives. The members also expected the same as well. They liked seeing the pastor working with her spouse as a team.

The husbands overwhelmingly agreed that the three things they liked best about being the pastor's husband were sitting at the head table at dinner functions, traveling, and meeting different people in various places. What they liked least about being the pastor's husband was sharing their wives with others. One other concern was whether or not roles are being confused in the home, and if this leads to marital conflict. The joint pastor least liked sharing the offerings. When asked what could better train them for the position of pastor's husband, they mentioned a closer relationship with the Lord, seminary training, more knowledge about the Bible and church decree, and patience. The husbands seemingly desire to better themselves and better serve their wives by improving spiritually and intellectually. This is an indication of selflessness.

The following results are presented according to the interviews: The respondents each serve in some type of leadership capacity, with the exception of one. These positions include trustee, deacon, superintendent of Sunday school, Sunday school teacher, musician, deacon board chairman, deacon board assistant chairman, Young

Folks and Friends Union president, Men's Auxiliary president, general elder, co-pastor, presiding elder, church administrator, treasurer, usher, and security officer. Only one said he does not hold a position presently.

One respondent stated there were no barriers in being a first husband. Others were concerned about late-night phone calls, which is understandable if they are working men. Some have experienced people shying away from them because of who they are (the pastor's husband). Yet another is cautious about forgetting his position in the church and taking control of situations when it is the wife's place. None of the husbands have spoken to the other first husbands from other denominations. Only one husband has spoken to another first husband within the House of God church. It is most likely this is something men just do not talk about.

Number fifteen on the survey questionnaire and question G on the interview questionnaire were synonymous. Responses obtained ultimately were the suggestions the men provided, which I thought to be considerations for their future roles. Anticipation of what these responses would render was worth the wait. The responses were categorized so as to compare which, if any, fell under leadership, mentorship, and brotherhood and to determine the husband's strongest attributes in fulfilling the role of "first gentleman." To my surprise, the husbands categorized a fourth trait of self-enrichment.

The following traits referenced their **leadership** skills:
- To help make joint decisions as co-pastors
- To work as a team
- To help schedule wife's meetings
- To serve as a deacon
- To serve as a trustee
- To share his experience and expertise with her when necessary
- To offer constructive suggestions to better the ministry
- To relieve her of stressful situations when possible
- To seek future theological training

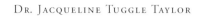

- To be obedient and first in following the pastor's lead
- To be an example before the members
- To follow close behind the deacon chairman
- To take a leadership role
- To have members follow the positive example of the pastor's husband so that everyone will fall in line
- To live an exemplary life so that other people will not stumble
- To motivate the members
- To give financially to the church
- To lead out
-

The following traits indicate **mentorship** skills:
-
- To share his experience and expertise with the wife
- To offer constructive suggestions to better the ministry
- To give advice

The following traits suggest **brotherhood** skills:

- To provide moral support and spiritual help and be a loving husband at all times.
- To serve as chauffeur
- To be an armor bearer
- To be a helper
- To motivate the members
- To give financially to the church
- To communicate with others
- To have a good relationship with the wife
- To be reverenced by the wife
- To be godly, loving, humble
- To be available when the wife needs you
- To protect her from physical harm

This fourth trait that is evident of the husbands is the desire of **self-enrichment:**

- To have self-confidence by studying the Bible and church decree
- To seek future theological training
- To seek training in time management

It is quite evident from the desires and present positions of the husbands that the greatest skill they already possess is that of leadership: this is what a first husband should have. This is most likely why they and their wives are so compatible and are able to work as a team: both are leaders in their specific callings. Communicating with others falls under brotherhood. This is the second greatest skill in the role of the pastor's husband. Interacting with others is a part of a pastor's responsibility and duty.

Often, the husband is a liaison between the people and the wife. It stands to reason that the skill of mentorship is one of the skills they will use least. Counseling in the church is primarily conducted by the pastor. Most likely, the husbands feel this way. In fact, one of the husbands mentioned in the interview that he leaves that up to his wife. Surprisingly enough, the husbands did address the desire to improve themselves in order to be better able to support their spouses.

The husbands were provided with nineteen traits and were asked to identify which best described their wives. Of the five husbands answering this question, four wives displayed more masculine traits than feminine traits as pastors. This is a positive indication that they will be successful leading both males and females. When asked what word or phrase best describes their wives, the husbands used terms like *aggressive, straightforward, prayerful, spiritually anointed, firm but fair,* and *persistent.* From personal experience, I can say that all of these characteristics are needed in shepherding a church, whether you are male or female.

One respondent felt that the husband should be a deacon, trustee, or musician; the other husbands felt it was up to God to lead the pastor to appoint them to appropriate positions.

Three of the husbands felt that when the wives are honored at an appreciation, they too should be honored with gifts and verbal recognition because they work along with the wives. One husband contends that the husband should not be recognized because it is the wife's day. Another husband said it should be up to the membership.

Reflections on Respondents' Recommendations

Overall, the husbands were divided when asked if their lives would be different if they were certain what their role as first husband would require. One said he would be more confident. Two husbands said there would be no difference. Two said it would be better. Apparently, one can better carry out one's responsibilities when one knows what is expected of one. The husbands refused to rate their performance in their present role as first husband. They avoided explaining why; therefore, we continued on with the interview. When asked, "In the future, would you like to be referred to as the 'first gentleman'?", all but one said yes. The one exception said he would rather remain the pastor's husband because the title is not that important and the husband should remain humble. Also, for so long the female spouses have been called "first lady," and he would rather not start anything new.

In conclusion, the men provided an additional list of the roles of the pastor's husband. Primarily, they are centered on their commitment in serving God, the church, wife, and others. They are as following:

- **Service to God:** Obedience to the Word of God; living a Christian life.
- **Service to the Church:** Active church attendance; doing all they can when called upon; serving faithfully as a deacon, trustee, usher, treasurer, or musician: evangelizing and spreading the good news; cleaning the church; cooking food to feed the kids after Sunday school.
- **Service to Wife:** Being her reader; working as a team; exposure to religious training to assist wife more;

presenting her to the congregation when she is giving a workshop; being her armor bearer; being supportive; providing her with suggestions, feedback to make things better; speaking positively in her absence; being available for her; coordinating travel and meetings for her; and being chauffeur.

- **Service to Others**: Being hospitable and showing respect to others as any other Christian; communicating to members on wife's behalf and encouraging others to come to her meetings.

It is apparent that these traits confirm that the husband's role falls under leadership, mentorship, brotherhood, and self-enrichment. It is evident that these husbands contemplated what their role should consist of. Their role is consistent with the following biblical characteristics of Lapidoth/Barak, Shallum, Joseph, and Aquila:

- Avoided patriarchal conflicts by allowing wife to fulfill her calling by God
- Believed in God and His purpose for his wife
- Did not interfere with wife's ministerial vocation
- Was industrious by being employed in the temple or self-employed
- Was faithful to God and wife
- Loved wife
- Respected wife's relationship with God
- Supported wife
- Was faithful in church attendance
- Communicated with God

The biblical husbands also have commonalities with roles presented in this study by Wright, Daniel, and Morgan. Indeed, this study accurately reflects the pastors and their husbands exemplified in the House of God Church. The role recommended by these husbands makes this ethnographic study valid and reliable. The result of the role of the female pastor's husband is typical of what the Scriptures have identified in other husbands of women in leadership positions. The role is also typical of what the men from the AME Conference presented. The husbands indeed exemplify servant leadership.

Conclusion

Reflexivity

When I began this project, I intended to cautiously conduct the research, especially because I am one of the administrators of the church. I reiterated to the husbands to respond honestly and to the best of their abilities and not to please me or respond in a way they thought I would like of them. I found that the use of countertransference[208] enabled me to have a closer connectedness with the husbands. The effectiveness of the brief pastoral strategies theory used as the method in developing the survey and interview questions led to the husbands taking ownership in defining their role as "first gentleman." It also established rapport and assured the husbands that the time taken to listen to their stories demonstrated that, as an official in the church, I was concerned about their journey and the transformation that needed to take place in their lives. Their role as husband to a female pastor is in no light humiliating, but it is significant in being a co-laborer when carrying out the work of the ministry.

With the exception of the husbands not responding to question E on the interview form, I did not sense any hesitancy, nor was there any indication of stress. The participants of this study were Attentive, patient, humble, and demonstrated their willingness to effect change even in their anonymity. The support of the wives was refreshing as they eagerly awaited a new challenge for their

---

[208] Cooper-White, vii.

husbands to pursue. I contend that the choices I made in selecting the appropriate ethnographic tools were sufficient in verifying the validity and reliability of accurate findings.

Conclusion and Reflections on Findings

The continuous theological debate concerning gender equity has prevailed for an undisclosed numbers of centuries, although theologians try to estimate its origin. This debate directly affected my research: if God does call women to ministry, it is logical that some women will become pastors and bishops as well as other leading administrators in the church, synagogue, mosque, etc. Married women who acknowledge being called by God to minister to the young and old, rich and poor, male and female of all nations and creeds have husbands who do not discriminate according to gender. This being the case, it opens an avenue for roles of the men in these anointed women's lives to evoke reality in mankind that God is a God of equality. This equality applies to gender, age, profession, economics, and ethnic culture today, and it is more prevalent for discussion in our ever-changing world. The presence of gender inequality has directly affected marital roles of husbands and wives from the patriarchal system of dominant rule to a more egalitarian system.

The interpretation of Scriptures by pre-modern and contemporary theologians concerning the sayings of the apostle Paul and the women's role in the church presented a concise picture that God uses whom He pleases and when He pleases to carry out His ultimate will.

Martos and Hégy support women in ministry and state, "Gender roles are an efficient social mechanism for ensuring group survival; when all know their place, the group functions well. Gender roles are also an efficient means of providing individual satisfaction: when everyone knows his or her place, individuals have a sense of belonging and purpose."[209] Indeed, recognition of male spouses will undoubtedly add to the husband's self-esteem. Recognition in the role of the female pastor's husband will change the dynamics of the

---

[209]   Martos and Hégy, 14.

church to acknowledge each person's calling by God and to respect that individual's ministry. We are exhorted to give honor to whom honor is due. When we think of the husband and wife, they are a team, unified in holy marriage, which was instituted by God in the beginning. When one spouse is happy, the other spouse should be happy. When one spouse is distraught, the other spouse should be a motivator and encourager to lift the spouse's spirits.

The roles of both husband and wife are clearly defined in the Scriptures as well as the role of particular men and women called by God to perform specific tasks. In this study, a review of the literature concerning the theological debate as to whether or not women should be deacons, pastors, elders, bishops, or holders of other leadership positions in the church has been solidified. The role of the husband is succinctly presented in the case studies presented in the lives of Deborah and Barak (Lapidoth), Huldah and Shallum, Mary and Joseph, and Priscilla and Aquila. Note that these husbands of women in leadership positions also held leadership positions when working with their wives in ministry. Therefore, the findings from this study of the role of the female pastor's husband can be classified under the categories of leadership, mentorship, brotherhood, and self-enrichment based on the responses of the husbands' perception of their role and what we have identified of the biblical husbands.

The ecclesiological aspects of religion must be discussed with those in patriarchal organizations toward a more egalitarian system. This is mainly due to major differences in characteristics of male and female pastors. The argument as to the leadership positions of women in the church definitely affects the leadership structure of the church. There is no doubt that this project will be an eye-opener for males and females who hold onto the myths concerning women not being called by God to leadership positions.

The conclusion of the whole matter is reiterated by Charles Johnson: "Women are submitting themselves to the call of God on their lives.[210] The Holy Spirit is the one calling women, and they

---

[210] Johnson, 492-493.

are responding to His call in record number to proclaim the gospel of Jesus Christ." Johnson also states that the will of God is that He intentionally plans to fill His pulpits with women as well as men.[211]

The ten men who participated in this study have clearly defined the role of the female pastor's husband in the House of God Church, Pentecostal Holiness denomination. I have no reservations in addressing my husband as "the first gentleman" of the local church. The title, with all its dignity, honor, humility, and obedience to God, demonstrates the love and support the husband has for his wife, "the pastor." Amen.

Discussion of Future Uses and Implications of Project Findings

In summary, this project was focused from a male perspective on the role of the first husband. Findings of the data collected was analyzed and shared in a public presentation with the husbands, their wives, and all interested parties. I facilitated the seminar titled "The Role of the Female Pastor's Husband" which was held at my home church in Essex, Maryland. Spouses as well as the church community demonstrated an understanding of what was expected of the male spouses of female pastors in the question and answer period which followed the workshop. In the future, a pocket manual with the description of the role of the "first gentleman" provided by the husbands can be developed and made available to interested parties.

The findings will also be presented to the House of God Church Supreme Executive Council for adoption of written guidelines in recognition of the role of the female pastor's husband. Also, it will be suggested to the Council to establish conferences that will address the concerns of ministers, spouses, and youth, as in the AME. Hopefully, the respondents' answers will set a precedent for future generations in studying the ecclesiological culture of religion, especially at their particular church to foster transformation.

---

[211] Ibid.

Lastly, it is greatly anticipated that religious institutions, seminaries, colleges, women study groups and organizations, and other non-religious venues will use this study as a point of reference in recognizing women (single or married) in leadership positions in a patriarchal society in an effort to transform to a more egalitarian society.

Recommendations and Next Steps for Future Study

Based on the responses from the interviews and surveys, here are some possible recommendations for future consideration of studies:

- The role of the female pastor's husband from a female perspective
- The role of the male pastor's wife from a male perspective
- The role of the male pastor's wife from a female perspective
- A longitudinal study two to three years after the completion of the aforementioned
- A comparative study four to five years after the longitudinal study

The content of this project study is intended for publication in journal magazines and to be published in book form. The reliability of this study is worth sharing in other venues within and without the religious culture.

BIBLIOGRAPHY
(Turabian 7th Edition)

Akin, Daniel L. *The New American Commentary: Volume 38, 1, 2, 3 John.*Nashville, Tennessee: Broadman & Holman Publishers, 2001.

Alexander, Estrelda Y. "Gender and Leadership in the Theology and Practice of Three Pentecostal Women Pioneers (Mary Magdalena Lewis Tate, Aimee Semple McPherson, Ida Robinson)." PhD dss., The Catholic University of America, Abstract DAI 63 no.12A (2003): 4345.

Anderson, Herbert, Don S. Browning, Ian S. Evison, and Mary Stewart Van Leeuwen, eds. *The Family Handbook.* Louisville, Kentucky: Westminister John Knox Press, 1998.

Anderson, John L. 1, 2, 3, John. Dallas: Summer Institute of Linguistics, 1992.

Bass, Bernard and Ruth. *The Bass Handbook of Leadership: Theory, Research and Managerial Applications. Fourth Edition.* New York, New York: Free Press, 2008.

Benvenuti, Sherilyn. "Anointed, Gifted and Called: Pentecostal Women in Ministry." *Pneuma* 17 no. 2 (Fall 1995): 229-235.

Blessing, Carol. "Judge, Prophet, Mother: Learning from Deborah." *Daughters of Sarah* 21 no. 1 (Wint 1995): 34-37.

Bolker, Joan. *Writing Your Dissertation in Fifteen Minutes a Day.* New York, New York: Henry Holt & Company, 1998.

Bristow, John Temple. *What Paul Really Said About Women: An Apostle's Liberating Views on Equality in Marriage, Leadership, and Love with Study Questions.* New York, New York: Harpers Collins, 1988.

Brown, Chip. "Hatshepsut—Ruled Egypt Twenty-One Years as a Man,1479-1458 B.C." *National Geographic.* 215 no. 4 (April 2009: 88-111).

Brown, Raymond E. The Epistles of John. Anchor Bible. New York, New York: Doubleday, 1992.

Butler, Trent C., Marsha A. Ellis Smith, Forrest W. Jackson, Phil Logan, and Chris Church. *Holman Bible Dictionary.* Nashville, Tennessee: Holman Bible Publishers, 1991.

Carter, Weptanomah W. *The Black Minister's Wife: as a Participant in the Redemptive Ministry of Her Husband.* Baltimore, Maryland: Gateway Press, Inc., 1995.

Charles, Sylvia. *Couples in the Bible: Examples to Live By.* Tulsa, Oklahoma:Hensley Publishing, 1998.

Christian Century. "Women in Ministry" 116 no. 7 (Mar 3, 1999): 239-240. [accessed June 30, 2010]

Cody-Rydzewski, Susan. "Married Clergy Women: How They Maintain Traditional Marriage Even As They Claim New Authority." *Review of Religious Research* 48 no. 3 (2007): 273-289.

Coogan, Michael D. *The Old Testament: A Historical and Literary Introduction to the Hebrew Scriptures.* New York, New York: Oxford University Press, 2006.

Comay, Joan and Ronald Brownrigg. *Who's Who in the Bible.* Avenel, New Jersey:Wings Books, 1980.

Cooper-White, Pamela. *Many Voices: Pastoral Psychotherapy in Relational and Theological Perspective.* Minneapolis, Minnesota: Fortress Press, 2006.

_____ *Shared Wisdom: The Use of the Self in Pastoral Care and Counseling* Minneapolis, Minnesota: Augsburg Fortress, 2004.

Copenhaver, Martin B. "Mixed Marriage: A Pastor and a Skeptic." *Christian Century* (July 14, 2009). *http://newfirstsearch.oclc.org/ WebZ/FSQUERY?format=BI:next=html/records.html:bad=html/ records.html:numrecs=10:sessionid=fsapp4-56801-gb14apnd d0hir:entitypagenum=44:0: searchtype=basic* [accessed May 15, 2010].

Cornwall, Judson and Stelman Smith. *The Exhaustive Dictionary of Bible Names.* Gainesville, Florida: Bridge—Logos, 1998.

Culbertson, Philip. *Caring for God's People: Counseling and Christian Wholeness.* Minneapolis, Minnesota: Fortress Press, 2000.

Culy, Martin M. *I, II, III John: A Handbook on the Greek Text.* Waco, Texas: Baylor University Press, 2004.

Daniel, Lillian. "The Pastor's Husband: Redefining Expectations." *Christian Century* 126 no 14 (July 14, 2009): 28-31. *http:// newfirstsearch.oclc.org/ WebZ/FSQUERY? format=BI:next=html/ records. html:bad=html/ records.html:numrecs=10:sessionid=fsapp4- 56801-gb14apnd-d0hir:entitypagenum=24:0:searchtype=basic* [accessed May 24, 2010].

Dart, John. "Female Pastors' Story Rattles SBC Nerves" *Christian Century* 125 no.21 (Oct 21 2008): 16-17 _*http:// newfirstsearch.oclc.org/WebZ/ FTFETCH? sessionid=fsapp6- 51254-:entitypagenum=21:0:rule=100: fetchtype=fulltext: dbname=ATLA_FT:recno=7:resultset=2:ftformat= PDF:forma t=BI:isbillable=TRUE:numrecs=1:isdirectarticle=FALSE:entitye mailfullrecno=7:entityemailfullresultset=2:entityemailftfrom=AT LA_FT:* [accessed May 24, 2010].

Deen, Edith. *All of the Women of the Bible.* New York, New York: HarperOne, 1983.

Deming, Laura. "The Two-Career Marriage: Implications for Ministry." *Word & World* 4, no. 2 (Spr 1984): 173-181. *http://newfirstsearch.oclc.org/WebZ/ FSFETCH?fetchtype=fullrecord:sessionid=fsapp6-51254-gb2iiz2q-fbvlk7:entitypagenum=141:0:recno=33:resultset=5:format=FI:next=html/record.html:bad=error/badfetch.html:entitytoprecno=33:entitycurrecno=33:numrecs=1* [accessed May 24, 2010].

Dieter, Melvin. *Great Holiness Classics: Volume Four The 19th-Century Holiness Movement.* Kansas City, Missouri: Beacon Hill Press of Kansas City, 1998.

Doniger, Simon. "Patterns of Stress and Support." *Pastoral Psychology* 55 no. 6 (July 2007). 761-771 *http://newfirstsearch.oclc.org/WebZ/ FSFETCH? fetchtype=fullrecord: sessionid=fsapp6-51254-gb2iiz2q fbvlk7:entitypagenum= 141:0:recno=33:resultset= 5:format= FI:next= html/record.html: bad=error/badfetch.html:entitytoprecno=33: entity currecno=33:numrecs=1* [accessed May 15, 2010].

Draper Jr., James T. *1 & 2 Thessalonians: The Hope of a Waiting Church.* Wheaton, Illinois: Tyndale House Publishers, Inc, 1971.

Dykstra, Robert C. *Images of Pastoral Care: Classic Readings.* St. Louis, Missouri: Chalice, 2005.

Easton, Matthew. "Deborah." Edited by Paul S. Taylor. *http://www.christiananswers.net/dictionary/deborah.html* [accessed July 2, 2010].

Ferrara, Dennis Michael. "The Ordination of Women: Tradition and Meaning." *Theological Studies* 55 no. 4 (Dec 1994): 706-719. *http://newfirstsearch.oclc.org/WebZ/ FSQUERY? format=BI:next=html/records.html:bad=html/ records.html:numrecs =10:sessionid=fsapp4-56801-gb14apnd 0hir:entitypagenum=55:0: searchtype=basic*

Fox, Curtis A, Priscilla W. Blanton, and M. Lane Morris. "Empirical Studies from Geography, History, Psychology, and Sociology-Religious Problem-Solving Styles: Three Styles Revisited."

Journal for the Scientific Study of Religion 37 no. 4 (1998): 673 (5 pages).

Galek, Kathleen, Kevin J. Flannelly, Martha R. Jacobs and John D. Barone. "Spiritual Needs: Gender Differences Among Professional Spiritual Care Providers." *Journal of Pastoral Care & Counseling* 62 no. 1-2 (Spr-Sum 2008): 29-35.

George, Elizabeth. *Cultivating a Life of Character: Judges/Ruth.* Eugene, Oregon: Harvest House Publishings, 2002.

Grady, J. Lee. *25 Tough Questions about Women and the Church.* Lake Mary, Florida: Charisma House, 2003.

Grasham, Bill. "The Role of Women in the American Restoration Movement." *Restoration Quarterly* 41 no. 4 (1999): 211-239. *http://newfirstsearch. oclc.org/WebZ/ FTFETCH?sessionid=fsapp7-51492-gb2n7l7l-vcvzx9:entitypagenum=3:0:rule=100:fetchtype=f ulltext:dbname=ATLA_ FT:recno=1:resultset=1:ftformat=PDF:fo rmat=BI:isbillable= TRUE:numrecs=1:isdirectarticle=FALSE:ent ityemailfullrecno=1:entityemailfullresultset=1:entityemailftfrom= ATLA_FT:* [accessed May 24, 2010].

Griswold, Phoebe W. "Living the Theology of a Bishop's Spouse: Experience, Experiment, and Adventure." *Angelican Theological Review* 81 no.1 (Winter 1999): 83-93. *http://findarticles.com/p/ articles/mi_qa3818/is 199901/ai_ n8844895/?tag=content;col1.* [accessed May 15, 2010].

Haines, Maxine L. *This Ministry We Share: A Manual for the Wesleyan Pastor's Wife.* Marion, Indiana: The Wesley Press, 1986.

Hammond, Michelle McKinney. *In Search of the Proverbs 31 Man: the One God Approved and a Woman Wants.* Colorado Springs, Colorado.:Waterbrook Press, 2003.

Harris, W. Hall III *1, 2, 3 John Comfort and Counsel for a Church in Crisis* Biblical Studies Press, 2003.

Hartung, Bruce M. Identity, the Pastor, and the Pastor's Spouse. *Theology and Mission*. 3 no.5 (October 1976), 307-311. *http:// newfirstsearch.oclc.org/WebZ/FTFETCH? sessionid=fsapp4-50542-gb1437a1 supir6:entitypagenum=3:0:rule= 100:fetchtype= fulltext:dbname=ATLA_FT:recno=1:resultset=1:ftformat= PDF:f ormat=BI:isbillable=TRUE:numrecs=1:isdirectarticle=FALSE:ent ityemailfullrecno=1:entityemailfullresultset=1:entityemailftfrom= ATLA_FT:* [accessed May 15, 2010].

Hirsch, Emil G and E. I. Nathans. *Lapidoth (Lappidoth). http://www. jewishencyclopedia.com/view.jsp?artid=69&letter-L&search=* Deborah [accessed July 2, 2010]

Hirsch, Emil G and E. I. Nathans, Wilhelm Bacher and Louis Ginzberg. *Shallum. http://www.jewishencyclopedia.com/view.jsp?artid=541& letter =S&search=shallum* [accessed July 2, 2010].

Hirsch, Emil G., Gerson B. Levi, Solomon Schechter, and Kaufmann Kohler. "Deborah." *http://www.jewishencyclopedia.com/view_ friendly.jsp?artid=187&letter=D* [accessed July 2, 2010].

Hirsch, Emil G, M. Seligsohn, Executive Committee of the Editorial Board and Louis Ginzberg. "Huldah" *http://www. jewishencyclopedia.com/view _friendly.jsp?artid=955&letter=H* [accessed July 2, 2010].

h*ttp://www.bible-people.info/Deborah.htm* "Deborah: Never Say Die! [accessed July 2, 2010].

h*ttp://www.christiananswers.net/dictionary/aquila.html* "Aquila."[accessed July 2, 2010]. h*ttp://www.christiananswers. net/dictionary/barak.html* "Barak." [accessed July 2, 2010]. h*ttp:// www.christiananswers.net/dictionary/deborah.html* "Deborah" [accessed July 2, 2010]. h*ttp://www.christiananswers.net/ dictionary/huldah.html* "Huldah" [accessed July 2, 2010]. h*ttp:// www.christiananswers.net/dictionary/lapidoth.html* "Lapidoth." [accessed July 2, 2010]. h*ttp://www.christiananswers.net/ dictionary/priscilla.html* "Priscilla." [accessed July 2, 2010]. h*ttp://*

www.christiananswers.net/dictionary/shallum.html "Shallum." [accessed July 2, 2010]. h*ttp://www.jewishencyclopedia.com/ view.jsp?artid=69&letter=L&search=* Deborah [accessed July 2, 2010].

http://www.jewishvirtuallibrary.org/jsource/biography/deborah. html "Deborah." [accessed July 2, 2010]. h*ttp://www. womeninthebible.net/1.8.Deborah_Jael.htm* "Deborah and Jael: Bible Women, Bible Warriors. Heroines Who Would Never Say Die!" [accessed July 2, 2010].

Husbands, Mark and Timothy Larsen, eds. *Women, Ministry, and the Gospel: Exploring New Paradigms.* Downers Grove, Illinois: IVP Academics, 2007.

Ironside, H. A. *Epistles of John & Jude. Revised Edition.* New Jersey: Loizeaux Neptune, 2001.

James, Carolyn Custis. *Lost Women of the Bible: Finding Strength & Significance through Their Stories.* Grand Rapids, Michigan: Zondervan, 2005.

Jarvis, Peter. "Men and Women Ministers of Religion." *Modern Churchman 22 no. 4 (1979): 149-158. http://newfirstsearch. oclc.org/WebZ/FSQUERY?   format=BI:next=html/records. html:bad=html/records.html:numrecs=10:sessionid   =fsapp4- 56801-gb14apndd0hir:entitypagenum=46:0: searchtype=basic.* [accessed June 29, 2010].

Jastrow, Morris, Jr, John Dyneley, Marcus Jastrow and Louis Ginzberg. "Barak" *http://www.jewishencyclopedia.com/view_ friendly.jsp?artid=267&leter=B* [accessed July 2, 2010]

Johnson, Charles F. "God's Women." *Review and Expositor* 103 no. 3 (Sum 2006): 491-493. *http://newfirstsearch.oclc.org/WebZ/ FTFETCH? sessionid=fsapp7-51492-gb2nc1mk-jhhshj:entitypa genum=8:0:rule=100: fetchtype=fulltext:dbname= ATLA_FT: recno=10:resultset=1:ftformat= PDF:format=BI:isbillable=TRU*

E:numrecs=1:isdirectarticle=FALSE:entityemailfullrecno=10:ent ityemailfullresultset=1:entityemailftfrom=ATLA_FT: [accessed June 30, 2010].

Josephus, Flavius, William Whiston, and Syvert Havercamp. *Complete Works of Josephus. Antiquities of the Jews; The Wars of the Jews Against Apion, etc., Volume One.* New York, New York: Bigelow, Brown & Co., Inc., before 1923.

Karras, Valerie A. "'Priestesses or Priests' Wives: Presbytera in Early Christianity." *St Vladimir's Theological Quarterly* 51 no. 2-3 (2007): 321-345.

Keith, Mary F. L. *Female Leadership Defended.* The Holy Bible (KJV). Specifically designed for the House of God Church, Inc. Nashville, Tennesee: Royal Publishers, Inc., before 1962, reprint 1971.

Keller, Marie Nöel. *Priscilla and Aquila*: Paul's Coworkers in Christ Jesus. Collegeville, Minnesota: Liturgical Press, 2010.

Kim, Eunjoo Mary. "The Holy Spirit and New Marginality." *Journal for Preachers* 25 No. 4 Pentecost (2002): 26-31. http:// newfirstsearch.oclc.org/WebZ/FTFETCH? sessionid=fsapp7- 51492-gb2nwhtl-xvxqer:entitypagenum=3:0:rule= 100:fetchtype= fulltext:dbname=ATLA_FT:recno=1:resultset= 1:ftformat= PDF:format=BI:isbillable=TRUE:numrecs=1:isdire ctarticle=FALSE:entityemailfullrecno=1:entityemailfullresults et=1:entityemailftfrom=ATLA_FT: [accessed June 30, 2010].

Kostenberger, Andreas J., Thomas R. Schreiner, and H. Scott Baldwins, eds. *Women in the Church: A Fresh Analysis of I Timothy 2:9-15.* Grand Rapids, Michigan: Baker Books, 1995.

Kroeger, Richard Clark and Catherine Clark-Kroeger. *I Suffer Not a Woman: Rethinking I Timothy 2:11-15 in Light of Ancient Evidence.* Grand Rapids, Michigan: Baker Book House, 1992.

Kujawa-Holbrook, S. and Montagno, K. *Injustice and the Care of Souls: Taking Oppression Seriously in Pastoral Care.* Minneapolis, Minnesota: Fortress Press, 2009.

Larsen, Dale and Sandy. *Couples of the Old Testament: Nine Studies for Individuals or Groups.* Downers Grove, Illinois: InterVarsity Press, 2004.

Lee, Cameron. "Patterns of Stress and Support Among Adventist Clergy: Do Pastors and their Spouses Differ?" *Pastoral Psychology* 55 (2007):761-771.

Lee, Jung Young. *Marginality: The Key to Multicultral Theology.* Minneapolis, Minnesota: Fortress Press, 1995.

Lewis, Mcharry H. *Mary Lena Lewis Tate: "A Street Called Straight" (Acts 9:11) The Ten Most Dynamic and Productive Black Female Holiness Preachers of the Twentieth Century.* Nashville, Tennesee: The New and Living Way Publishing Company, 002.

Lin, Yu-Fen. "Self-Esteem of Female Pastors in Taiwan: the Development of the YFL Feminist Group Counseling Model for Asian Female Pastors." PhD dss., Sam Houston University, DAI 70 no. 08A (2009): 2903.

Lockyer, Herbert. *All the Men of the Bible: All the Women of the Bible.* Grand Rapids, Michigan: Zondervan, (All the Men of the Bible,1958), (All the Women of the Bible, 1967).

MacArthur, John, Jr. *The MacArthur New Testament Commentary: 1 & 2 Thessalonians.* Chicago, Illinois: Moody Press, 2002.

Martos, Joseph and Pierre Hégy, eds. *Equal at the Creation: Sexism, Society, and Christian Thought.* Toronto: University of Toronto Press, 1998.

Matthews, Lawrence. "Bowen Family Systems Theory: A Resource for Pastoral Theologians." *Review and Expositor* 102 (Summer 2005).

McMinn, Mark R, R. Allen Lish, Pamela D. Trice, Alicia M. Root, Nicole Gilbert, and Adelene Yap. "Care for Pastors: Learning from Clergy and Their Spouses." *Pastoral Psychology* 53 no. 6 (July 2005).

Mendiola, Kelly Willis. "*The Hand of a Woman: Four Holiness-Pentecostal Evangelists and American Culture, 1840-1930 (Phoebe Palmer, Amanda Smith, Mary Magdalena Lewis Tate, Aimee Semple McPherson, Oprah Winfrey).* Abstract, PhD diss., The University of Texas at Austin, DAI 64 no.12A (2002):4508.

Miller, Stephen M. *The Complete Guide to Bible Prophecy.* Phoenix, ArizonaBarbour Publishers, Inc, 2010.

_____*Who's Who and Where's Where in the Bible.* Uhrichsville, Ohio: Barbour Publishing Inc., 2004.

Minter, Ruth Brandon. "Women in Ministry: Beyond the Obstacles." *The Christian Ministry.* March 1985: 19-22.

Moon, Helena. "Womenpriests." *Journal of Feminist Studies in Religion 24 no 2 (2008):115-13 http://newfirstsearch.oclc.org/WebZ/ FTFETCH?sessionid=fsapp7-58740gb2p2ejorgvh4r:entitypagenu m=4:0:rule=100:fetchtype=fulltext:dbname=ATLA_FT:recno=3: resultset=1:ftformat=PDF:format=BI:isbillable=TRUE:numrecs=1 :isdirectarticle=FALSE:entityemailfullrecno=3:entityemailfullresul tset=1:entityemailftfrom=ATLA_FT:* [accessed June 30, 2010].

Morgan, Edward. "Implications of the Masculine and the Feminine in Pastoral Ministry." *Journal of Pastoral Care* 34 no. 4 (Dec 1980): 268-277.*http://newfirstsearch.oclc.org/WebZ/ FTFETCH?sessionid=fsapp6-51254 gb2iiz2q-fbvlk7:entitypagen um=243:0:rule=100:fetchtype=fulltext: dbname =ATLA_FT:re cno=12:resultset=10:ftformat= PDF:format=BI:isbillable=TRU E:numrecs=1:isdirectarticle=FALSE:entityemailfullrecno=12:ent ityemailfullresultset=10:entityemailftfrom=ATL_FT:* [accessed June 30, 2010].

Morris, Joan. *The Lady Was a Bishop: The Hidden History of Women with Clerical Ordination and the Jurisdiction of Bishops.* New York, New York: The Macmillan Co, 1973.

Morris, Michael L. and Priscilla Blanton. "Predictors of Family Functioning among Clergy and Spouses: Influences of Social Context and Perceptions of Work-Related Stressors." *Journal of Child and Family Studies* 7 no. 1 (1998): 27-41.

Moschella, Mary Clark. *Ethnography as a Pastoral Practice: An Introduction.* Pilgrim Press. Cleveland, Ohio: 2008.

Mulligan, Mary Alice. "Women with a Mission: Religion, Gender, and the Politics of Women Clergy." *Encounter* 68 no. 1 (Wint 2007): 90-103. *http://newfirstsearch.oclc.org/ WebZ/FSFETCH ?fetchtype=fullrecord:sessionid= fsapp7-60609-gb2ocwtl-6g04c1 :entitypagenum=3:0:recno=2:resultset= 1:format=FI:next=html/ record.html:bad=error/badfetch.html:entitytoprecno=2:entitycur recno=2:numrecs=1* [accessed June 30, 2010].

Oden, Marilyn Brown. "Stress and Purpose: Clergy Spouses Today." *Christian Century* 105 no. 13 (Apr 20, 1988): 402-404. *http://newfirstsearch.oclc.org/WebZ/ ?sessionid=fsapp6-51254-gb2iiz2q-fbvlk7:entitypagenum=133:0: rule=100:fetchty pe=fulltext:dbname=ATLA_FT:recno=14:resultset=5:ftformat= PDF:format=BI:isbillable=TRUE:numrecs=1: isdirectarticle=FA LSE:entityemailfullrecno=14:entityemailfullresultset=5:entityem ailftfrom=ATLA_FT:* [accessed May 24, 2010].

Randall, Kevin J. "Clergy Career Patterns: Is Leaving or Cleaving Different for Men and Women?" *Modern Believing* 48 no. 4 (Oct 2007): 10-19 *http://newfirstsearch. oclc.org/ WebZ/ FTFETCH?sessionid=fsapp7-60609-gb2omjyi bnevkv:entity pagenum=3:0:rule=100:fetchtype= fulltext:dbname=ATLA_ FT:recno=1:resultset=2:ftformat =PDF:format=BI:isbillable=TR UE:numrecs=1:isdirectarticle=FALSE:entityemailfullrecno=1:en tityemailfullresultset=2:entityemailftfrom=ATLA_FT* [accessed June 30, 2010].

Randall, Robert L. *The Eternal Triangle: Pastor, Spouse, and Congregation.* Minneapolis, Minnesota: Fortress Press, 1992.

Readon, Patrick Henry. "Judge Deborah: The Hebrew Prophetess in Christian Tradition. *Touchstone (US)* 13 no. 3 (Apr. 2000):18-25.

Richards, Sue and Larry Richards. *Every Woman in the Bible.* Nashville, Tennessee: Thomas Nelson Publishers, 1999.

_____ *Women of the Bible: The Life and Times of Every Woman in the Bible.* Nashville, Tennessee: Thomas Nelson, Inc., 2003.

Robbins, Mandy, Leslie J. Francis, John M. Haley, and William K. Kay. "The Personality Characteristics of Methodist Ministers: Feminine Men and Masculine Women?" *Journal for the Scientific Study of Religion* 40 no. 1 (Mar. 2001): 123-128. *fsapp4-56801-gb14apndhttp://newfirstsearch.oclc.org/WebZ/FSQUERY?format=BI:next= html/ records.html:bad=html/records. html:numrecs=10:sessionid= fsapp4-56801-gb14apnd-d0hir:entityp agenum=53:0:searchtype=basic* [accessed June 30, 2010].

Robinson, Bruce A. "Women as Religious Leaders in the Bible and Early Christian Writings." *Ontario Consultants on Religious Tolerance http://www.religioustolerance.org/femclrg.htm* updated September 26, 2008. [accessed July 1, 2010].

Rock, Stanley. "Marriage, Ministry and the Families That Shaped Us." *Family Ministry* 13 no.2 (Summer 1999).

Sevier, Mellisa Bane. "Support and Solidarity: How Clergywomen Create Healthy." *Congregations* 30 no. 3, 9 (Sum 2004): 25-28.

Scott, Stuart. *The Exemplary Husband: A Biblical Perspective Revised Edition.* Bemidji, Minnesota: Focus Publishing, Inc. 2002.

Smith, David L. "Some Thoughts on the Preserving of Clergy Marriages." *(Didaskalia Otterburne, Man)* 7 no.1 (Fall 1995): 61-65 *http:// newfirstsearch.oclc.org/ WebZ/FTFETCH?sessionid=fsapp7-*

*60609-gb2mkahx-rnqsh8:entitypagenum= 7:0:rule=100:fetchty pe=fulltext:dbname=ATLA_*

FT:recno=35:resultset=1:ftformat=PDF:format=BI:isbillable=TRUE:n umrecs=1:isdirectarticle=FALSE:entityemailfullrecno=35:entitye mailfullresultset=1:entityemailftfrom=ATLA_FT: [accessed May 24, 2010].

Soelle, Dorothee *Suffering.* Philadelphia, Pennsylvania: Fortress Press, 1975.

Stamps, Donald C. ED. *New International Version Life in the Spirit Study Bible.* 998-1000, Zondervan. Grand Rapids, Michigan: 1973.

Stone, Howard W., ed. *Strategies for Brief Pastoral Counseling.* Minneapolis, Minnesota: Fortress Press, 2001.

Sundby, Mark and Susan Nienaber. "The Truth beneath the Myths: What We Can Learn from a Study of Clergy Competencies." *Congregations* 35 no. 4 (Fall 2009): 18-21.

Svennungsen, Ann M. "When Women Lead the Flock." *Congregations* 30 no. 3 (Sum *2004): 21-24.*

Swinton, John and Mowat, Harriet. *Practical Theology and Qualitative Research.* London: SCM Press, 2006.

Tanakh the Holy Scriptures: The New JPS Translation According to the Traditional Hebrew Text. Philadelphia, Pennsylvania: The Jewish Publication Society, 1985.

The Constitution Government and Decree of the Church of the Living God, the Pillar and Ground of the Truth. Nashville, Tennessee The New and Living Way Publishing Co.,1989 Reprint.

The Harper Collins Study Bible: Including Apocryphal Deuterocanonical Books with Concordance. New York, New York: HarperOne, 2006.

The House of God 107th Annual General Assembly Program. Nashville, Tennessee: House of God Printers, June 2010.

The House of God Statistical Church Report. Annual meeting June 14, 2010,Nashville, Tennessee.

The New Interpreter's Study Bible: New Revised Standard Version with the Apocrypha. Nashville, Tennessee: Abingdon Press, 2003.

Trothen, Tracy J. "Through the Looking Glass" *Journal of Pastoral Care & Counseling* 59 no. 1-2 (Spr-Sum 2005): 29-42.

Turabian, Kate L. *A Manual for Writers of Research Papers, Theses, and Dissertations: Chicago Style for Students and Researchers*, Seventh Edition, Revised by Wayne C. Booth, Gregory G. Colomb, Joseph M. Williams, and University of Chicago Editorial Staff. Chicago and London: University of Chicago Press, 2007.

Walker, William O. "The Portrayal of Aquila and Priscilla in Acts: The Question of Sources" *New Testament Studies.* 54 no. 4 (2008): 479-495.

Wallace, Daniel. "Aquila and Priscilla 1 Corinthians 16:19." *http:// bible.org/article/aquila-and-priscilla-1-corinthians-1619* [accessed July 2, 2010].

Waweru, Humphrey Mwangi. "Jesus and Ordinary Women in the Gospel of John: an African Perspective." *Svensk missionstidskrift.* 96 no. 2 (2008): 139-159. *http://newfirstsearch.oclc.org/WebZ/ FTFETCH?sessionid=fsapp7-60609-gb2oxz47-xt9r35:entitypagen um=4:0:rule=100:fetchtype=fulltext:dbname= ATLA_FT:recno=1 :resultset=1:ftformat=PDF:format=BI:isbillable=TRUE:numrecs=1 :isdirectarticle=FALSE:entityemailfullrecno=1:entityemailfullresult set=1:entityemailftfrom=ATLA_FT:* [accessed June 30, 2010].

Wijk-Bos, Johanna W H. "I Am . . . . Biblical Women Tell Their Own Stories." *Journal of Family Ministry* 19 no. 2 (Sum 2005): 84-85. *http://newfirstsearch.oclc.org/WebZ/ FTFETCH?sessionid=fsapp7-*

*51492-gb2nj1al-kj27fz:entitypagenum= 7:0:rule=100:fetchtype= fulltext:dbname=ATLA_*

FT:recno=17:resultset=1:ftformat=PDF:format=BI:isbillable=TRUE:nu mrecs=1:isdirectarticle=FALSE:entityemailfullrecno=17:entityem ailfullresultset=1:entityemailftfrom=ATLA_FT: [accessed June 30, 2010].

Willhauck, Susan and Jacquelyn Thorpe. *The Web of Women's Leadership: Recasting Congregational Ministry.* Nashville, Tennessee: Abingdon Press, 2001.

Williams, Delores. *Sisters in the Wilderness, The Challenge of Womanist God-Talk.*Maryknoll, New York, New York: Orbis Books, 2004 ninth printing.

Williams, Melvin. *Conn-M-SWAWO Plus PK's.* "The Role of the Male Spouse." Baltimore, Maryland: Oct 2010.

Witte, John, Jr., M. Christian Green, and Amy Wheeler, eds. *The Equal-Regard Family and It's Friendly Critics: Don Browning and the Practical Theological Ethics of Family.* Grand Rapids, Michigan: William B. Eerdmans Publishing Company, 2007.

Wimberley, Edward P. *African American Pastoral Care and Counseling: The Politics Of Oppression and Empowerment.* Cleveland, Ohio: The Pilgrim Press, 2006.

_____ *Counseling African American Marriages and Families.* Louisville, Kentucky: Westminster John Knox Press, 1997.

_____ *Recalling Our Own Stories: Spiritual Renewal for Religious Caregivers.* San Francisco, California: Jossey-Bass Publishers, 1997.

_____ *Using Scripture in Pastoral Counseling.* Nashville, Tennessee: Abingdon Press, 1994.

Women of Destiny Bible: Women Mentoring Women through the Scriptures. Nashville, Tennessee: Thomas Nelson Publishers, 2000.

Wooley, Matt and Julie. *Till Ministry Us Do Part?* Leadership, Spring 2004.

Wright, Jim. "Notes from a Pastor's Husband." *Christian Ministry* 17 no 1 (Ja 1986):12.

Youngblood, R. F., Herbert Lockyer, Sr., F. F. Bruce, and R. K. Harrison, eds.*Nelson's New Illustrated Bible Dictionary.* Nashville, Tennessee: Thomas Nelson Publishers,1995.Zikmund, Barbara Brown. "Women, Men, and Styles of Clergy Leadership." *Christian Century* 115 no. 14 (My 6 1998): 478-480, 482-486. *http://newfirstsearch. oclc.org/ WebZ/FTFETCH?sessionid=fsapp7-58740-gb2n2dsb-5av7c4:entitypagenum=3:0:rule=100:fetch type=fulltext:dbname=ATLA_FT:recno=1:resultset=1:ftform at=PDF:format=BI:isbillable=TRUE:numrecs=1:isdirectartic le=FALSE:entityemailfullrecno=1:entityemailfullresultset=1: entityemailftfrom=ATLA_FT:* [accessed June 30, 2010].

Zondag, Hessel J. "Unconditional Giving and Unconditional Taking: Empathy and Narcissism among Pastors." *Journal of Pastoral Care & Counseling.* 61 no. 1-2 (Spr-Sum 2007), 85-97. *http:// newfirstsearch.oclc.org/WebZ/FSQUERY? format=BI:next= html/ records.html:bad=html/records.html:numrecs=10: sessionid=fsapp 4-56801-gb14apnd-d0hir:entitypagenum=50:0: searchtype=basic.* [accessed June 29, 2010].

ROLE OF BIBLICAL HUSBANDS
OF FEMALE LEADERS

LAPIDOTH/ BARAK	SHALLUM	JOSEPH	AQUILA
Admired wife	Advised wife	A praying man	Avoided
Advised wife	Agreeable	Adopted wife's	patriarchal
Avoided	Avoided	child born of God	conflicts
patriarchal	patriarchal	Avoided	Co-Pastor
conflicts	conflicts	patriarchal	Encouraged,
Believed in her	Believed in her	conflicts	supported and
God given talents	God given talents	Believed in God	challenged wife
Courageous	Did not interfere	and His purpose	Faithful to God
Industrious-	with wife's	for his wife	and wife
Employed in the	ministry	Caring	Had a zeal for
Temple	Encouraged wife	Fair	Christ
Encouraged wife	Industrious-	Faithful to God	Honest Business
Enlightened	Employed in the	and wife	reputation
Faithful to God	Temple	Good	Hospitable
and wife	Faithful to God	Humble	Industrious—self
Inseparable from	and wife	Industrious—self	employed as a
wife	Leader in the	employed as a	tent maker
Leader in the	Temple	carpenter	Inseparable from
military	Loved wife	Keeper of the	wife
Loved wife	Obedient to God	Law	Keeper of the
Modest	Patient	Kind	Law
Obedient to God	Pious	Leader in the	Leader in the
Pious	Protector of	community	community
Poet	family	Loved God, wife	Loved God and
Proud of wife's	Provider	and family	wife
accomplishments		Not jealous	Obeyed God

Protector	Respected wife's	Not vindictive	Oneness with
Respected wife's	relationship with	Obedient to God	God, wife and
relationship with	God	Patient	fellowman
God	Sensitive	Pious	Studious
Supported wife	Supported wife	Protector of	Trusting
Sympathetic	Taught sons a	family	Missionized
Team player	trade	Provider	Not jealous of
Trustworthy	Unselfish	Respected wife's	wife
Valiant	Waited upon	relationship with	Religious
Worked as a team	God	God	Righteous
with wife		Sensitive	Secure
		Supported wife	Supported wife in
		Taught sons a	her ministry
		trade	Teacher
		Unselfish	Preacher
		Waited upon	Worked as a team
		God	with wife

116

Survey Questionnaire

Part I. Demographics

Please check the box beside your appropriate age group:

1. _____ 21-30 years of age _____ 31-40 years of age

   _____ 41-50 years of age _____ 51-60 years of age

   _____ 61-70 years of age _____ 71 and above

2. Your Race:

   _____

3. What Denomination were you before you married the Pastor:

   _____

4. How long have you been married to the Pastor? _____

5. Was your wife a pastor before you were married?
   _____ Yes _____ No

6. How many years have you been married? _____

7. Have you been married previously? _____ Yes _____ No

8. Do you have school-age children? _____ Yes _____ No

9. What is your occupation? _____

   _____

Part II. Survey Questions:

10. How would you describe your role as the Pastor's husband?

11. What are your wife's expectations of you in the church?

12. What are the member's expectations of you as the Pastor's husband?

13. What do you like best about being the Pastor's husband?

14. What do you least about being the Pastor's husband?

15. What further training or experience do you think is needed to better prepare you in your role as the Pastor's husband?

INTERVIEW QUESTIONNAIRE

1. What other positions do you hold in the church presently?

2. What programs have you instituted in the church in your role as Pastor's husband?

3. How do you differentiate your roles as Pastor's husband, husband and member?

4. Have you mentored (counseled or given advice to) anyone in the church?

5. What is your theological belief concerning female pastors and bishops? What scriptures may come to mind to support your belief?

6. What is your perception of the role of the Pastor's husband presently?

7. Are there barriers of being a 1ˢᵗ husband? If so, explain what they are.

8. Have you discussed the role of the 1ˢᵗ husband with other 1ˢᵗ husbands in other denominations? If so, how did they describe their role?

9. Have you discussed the role of the 1ˢᵗ husband with other 1ˢᵗ husbands in the House of God Church? If so, how did they describe their role?

10. How would you define the role of the Pastor's husband for future considerations?

ADDITIONAL QUESTIONS

A. Which of the following characteristics describes your wife?

Check all that applies.

1. tenderness (gentleness, compassion, kindness) _____
2. capacity to penetrate (go through, break through, pierce) _____
3. sensitivity (feeling, warmth, understanding) _____
4. separate (disconnect, take apart, divide) _____
5. devious (tricky, scheming, underhanded) _____
6. take charge (take control, take over, assume responsibility) _____
7. seducer (one who leads somebody astray, win somebody over) _____
8. indefinite (vague, unclear, indistinct) _____

9. initiate (start, kickoff, instigate) _____
10. feeling (having emotions, sentimental, sensitive) _____
11. creative (original, inspired, artistic) _____
12. receptive (open, interested, friendly) _____
13. stands firmly over and against (unmovable, steadfast, determined) _____
14. elusive (hard to pin down, indescribable, mysterious) _____
15. articulates (communicate something, speak intelligibly, speak distinctly) _____
16. jealous (envious, resentful, desirous) _____
17. expressive (open, meaningful, significant) _____
18. yielding (soft, squashy, compliant)_____
19. understanding   (considerate, thoughtful, appreciative) _____
20. What one word or phrase best describes your wife?

    _____

B. Which positions should the pastor's husband hold in the church?

C. When the wife is honored in an anniversary or appreciation service should the husband also be honored? If so how?

D. How may your life be different, if you, as well as other's knew specifically what your role should entail?

E. Based on a scale of one to ten (1-10), would you change how you are perceived in your present role as the pastor's husband? What number would you choose?

F. Would you like to be recognized as First Husband in the future?

G. List at least three to five tangible things (able to be touched, able to be realized) that describe the role of the pastor's husband.

1.

2.

3.

4.

5.

SAMPLE GRID FOR INTERVIEW DATA ORGANIZATION

QUESTION	RESPONDENT #
1. What other positions do you hold in the church presently?	
2. What programs have you instituted in the church in your role as Pastor's husband?	
3. How do you differentiate your roles as Pastor's husband, husband and member?	
4. Have you mentored (counseled or given advice to) anyone in the church?	
5. Have you instituted any programs in the church?	
6. What is your theological belief concerning female pastors and bishops? What scriptures may come to mind to support your belief?	

7. Are there barriers of being a 1st husband? If so, explain what they are.	
8. Have you discussed the role of the 1st husband with other 1st husbands in other denominations? If so, how did they describe their role?	
9. Have you discussed the role of the 1st husband with other 1st husbands in the House of God Church? If so, how did they describe their role?	
10. How would you define the role of the Pastor's husband for future considerations?	

Letter to Research Participants

7906 Westmoreland Avenue
Baltimore, Maryland 21234
July 8, 2010

Dear House of God Research Participant:

Thank you for allowing me to survey and interview you for my research project. This is part of my project study in which I must complete in order to graduate May 2011 with my Doctor of Ministry Degree from Wesley Theological Seminary in Washington, D.C.

The project I have chosen to research is "The Role of the Female Pastor's Husband in the House of God Church—Pentecostal Holiness Denomination. As you are well aware, the church was founded by a woman and we have many female leaders. Spouses of male Pastors are often recognized and held in high esteem as the First Lady. To my knowledge there are no guidelines or recognition given to the husband's of female pastor's as First Gentleman or First Man. This survey will also benefit husbands and wives who co-pastor, or those whose wife is a bishop. With your assistance you can be trail blazers in helping to define the Role of the Female Pastor's Husband in the House of God Church.

Our Chief Overseer and my Prelate are aware of this project and has given me their blessings. They will never know who participated in the survey because I promise to keep your name confidential and "no one" besides myself will know of your participation.

Enclosed is a Consent Form explaining my project and the details concerning your anonymity. **Please sign and return to me in the enclosed stamped envelop by August 15, 2010.** Additionally, I have sent you a copy of survey questions and interview questions. If you are not available for a formal interview we may interview by phone, audio taping, email or US Postal services. If we conference by phone, I will be glad to record your responses for you electronically. You will be identified by a Respondent # in the study. Return the survey forms handwritten if you do not have access to a computer. If you prefer to conference and have me record for you, please advise me when we speak.

Your honest and willing participation hinges on the success of this project. My instructors have given me a limited time to submit this portion of my study to them. My goal is to complete the surveys and interviews by October 1, 2010. Thank you for your commitment and support in this new initiative in identifying the role of the First Husband in the House of God Church.

Your sister in Christ,

General Elder Jacqueline Taylor

Ethnographic Consent Form For Interviews

Introduction: My name is Jacqueline Mae Tuggle Taylor, and I am a student at Wesley Theological Seminary, in Washington, D.C. I am conducting an ethnographic study as partial fulfillment in obtaining a Doctor of Ministry degree. Ethnography is the study of how a people, a community, and or a culture practice their faith. This will enable pastoral caregiver's insight on how to better serve their congregants.

My telephone number at home is 410 663-8252; cell is 410 963-4851. My research professor is Dr. Lewis Parks and his phone number is 202-885-8600. You may contact either of us at any time if you have questions about this study.

Purpose: The purpose of this ethnographic research is to study the role of the female pastor's husband in the House of God Church. I am trying to determine how husbands of female pastors define their role as First Husband or First Man.

Procedure: If you consent to participate in this study, you will be asked several questions in an oral interview that will take place at an agreeable location with you. It may be by telephone conference, in person, Internet video conferencing, or U.S. postal mail system. An audiotape of the interview to ensure accuracy of information may be conducted with your permission. **Time required:** The interview will take 1-1 ½ hours of your time.

Voluntary participation: Your participation in this study is completely voluntary. If you choose to participate, you may still refuse to answer any question that you do not wish to answer. You may also withdraw from the study at any time.

Risks: There are no known risks associated with this interview. However, it is possible that you might feel distress in the course of the conversation. If this happens, please inform me promptly.

Benefits: While there is no guaranteed personal benefit, it is possible that you will have personal fulfillment in knowing that you have been proactive as a trail blazer in defining the role of the female pastor' husband. This study is also intended to benefit the House of God Church wherever it is established by setting a standard to be followed; also to be a tool that other denominations may use as a pattern if they so desire.

Confidentiality/Anonymity: Your name will be kept confidential in all of the reporting and/or writing related to this study. I will be the only person present for the interview and the only person who listens to the tapes. When I write the ethnography, I will use pseudonyms-made up names—for all participants, unless you specify in writing that you wish to be identified by name.

If you wish to choose your own pseudonym for the study, please indicate the first name you would like me to use for you here _____.

Sharing the results: I plan to construct an ethnography—a written account of what I learn—based on these interviews together with my reading and historical research. This portion of the ethnography research will be submitted to my research professor by October 1, 2010.

I plan to share what I learn from this portion of the ethnography study in a seminar titled, "The Role of the Female Pastor's Husband in the House of God Church—Pentecostal Holiness Denomination." Laity as well as ministers will participate in this research. In addition, portions of this study may be printed and made available to those in attendance of the seminar.

Publication: There is the possibility that I will publish this study or refer to it in published writings in the future. In this event, I will continue to use pseudonyms (as described above) and I may alter some identifying details in order to further protect your anonymity.

Before you sign: By signing below, you are agreeing or disagreeing to an audiotape interview for this research study. Check the appropriate box.

☐ I agree to an audio-taping.   ☐ I do not agree to an audio-taping.

Be sure that any questions you may have are answered to your satisfaction. If you agree to participate in this study, a copy of this document will be given to you.

Participant's Signature: _____

Date: _____

Print Name: _____

Researcher's Signature: _____

Date: __July 8, 2010___

Print Name: _____Jacqueline M. Tuggle Taylor_____

INSTITUTIONAL REVIEW BOARD APPLICATION ETHNOGRAPHIC RESEARCH PROTOCOL

1. Jacqueline Mae Tuggle Taylor, Researcher.
    Contact Home Phone #: 410 663-8252;
    Cell Phone #: 410 963-4851
    Wesley Theological Seminary, Washington, D.C.
    Dr. Lewis Parks, Research Professor
    Contact Voice Mail Number: 202-885-8600

2. This ethnographic research study is to define the Role of the Female Pastor's Husband in the House of God Church Pentecostal Holiness Denomination from a male perspective.

3. Ten pastor's husbands within the Church were observed. A survey was conducted to ascertain demographics. Interviews were conducted to measure success of the research and to determine the role of the female pastor's husband.

    The individuals were observed at least once during the study and one formal interview was also conducted. Documentation of their responses were noted in a field journal. Permission to audio tape was asked of the participants, however none of the men consented. The interviews lasted between one and one-half hours. A joint decision of location for the interviews was made between the researcher and participants.

4.   A culminating activity of a public presentation will facilitate dialogue of transformation. The seminar will be held at my church in Essex, Maryland and I will facilitate dialogue of transformation with an audience of clergy and laity. In conclusion, the survey and interview questions will be used to measure validity of the research.

5.   Attached is a copy of the Survey and Interview Questionnaires that were administered to the participants.

6.   Presently, I serve as General Elder of two of the participants in this study. The other participants are acquaintances of the church.

7.   This study is intended to benefit the church at-large by providing written guidelines for the role of female pastor's husbands. In addition,

8.   The husbands will be encouraged to seek fulfillment in their role through the re-authoring of their stories. The seminar will enable all to share their stories with others who in turn will become spiritually renewed.

9.   The only potential risk to this study is that the husbands may become extremely sensitive upon reflection of a question. During the interviews I listened to their concerns and demonstrated as much compassion and understanding as possible. Participants that had an adverse effect or concern was reassured of confidentiality and anonymity.

10. Honesty with the participants was of utmost importance. Participants were provided with a consent form which was reviewed with them concerning confidentiality/anonymity. Signatures of both participant and researcher validated consent to interview the participants. Pseudonyms or a numerical coding system was used for participants desiring anonymity. The respondent's in this study were assigned a number from

one to ten. Individuals who gave permission to be interviewed and use their names were identified in the study.

11. Data was stored electronically on a USB port. Hard copies from interviews were locked in a storage bin and will be maintained for three years, except in the case of use of materials for further research or writing of a book.

12. Attached is a copy of the consent form provided for those being interviewed.

13. The final results of the study will be shared with the husbands, their wives and the public for reflection and celebration. This information is being used for my project study at Wesley Theological Seminary.

TABLES

Table 3.1 Statistics of Female and Male Pastors in the HOGC

Total Number Of Churches	Female Pastors	Male Pastors
167	50%	50%
167	83	84

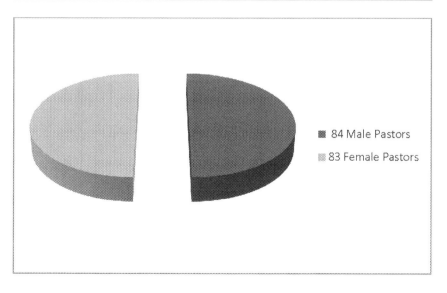

Table 3.2 Percentage of Female and Male Pastors in Dioceses

Total Number of Dioceses	Female Pastors	Male Pastors
24	13	11
24	50% More Female Pastors	50% More Male Pastors

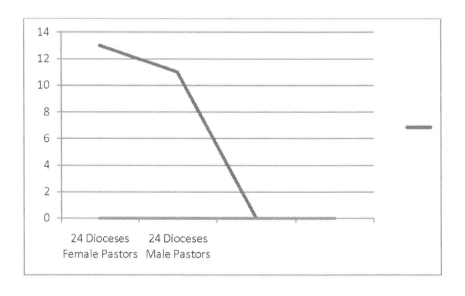

Table 4.1 Respondents Range of Age Range

41-50 Years	51-60 Years	61-70 Years	Over 71 Years
10%	10%	60%	20%
1 Respondent	1 Respondent	6 Respondents	2 Respondents

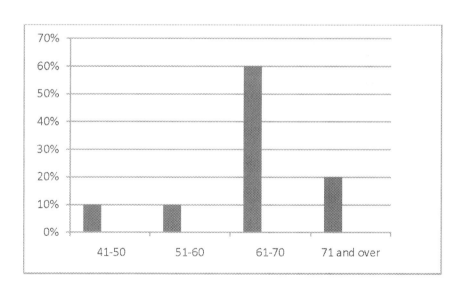

Table 4.2 Ethnicity of Respondents

African-American	Jamaican	African
80%	10%	10%
8 Respondents	1 Respondent	1 Respondent

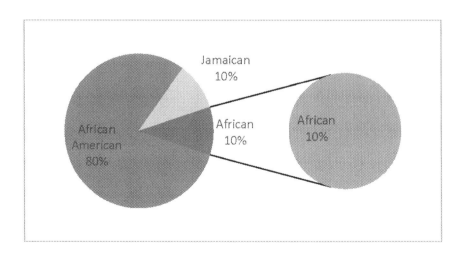

Table 4.3 Religious Denomination Prior to Marriage

Unchurched	COGIC	Apostolic	HOGC
10%	10%	10%	70%
1 Respondent	1 Respondent	1 Respondent	7 Respondents

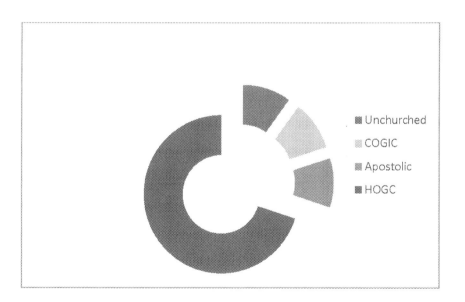

Table 4.4 Years Husbands Were Married to Wife as a Pastor

Respondents	Years
Respondent #1	25
Respondent #2	30
Respondent #3	16
Respondent #4	2
Respondent #5	30
Respondent #6	No Response
Respondent #7	12
Respondent #8	7
Respondent #9	13
Respondent #10	8

Table 4.5 Years Wife Was a Pastor Before Marriage

Wife Pastored before Marriage	Wife Pastored after Marriage
10%	90%
1 Respondent	9 Respondents

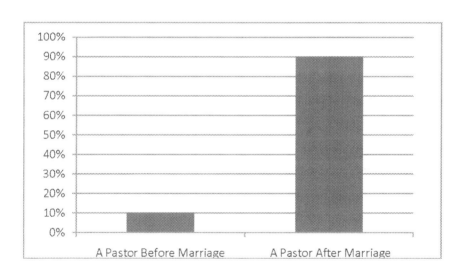

Table 4.6 Total Years Husband Married to Wife

Respondents	Total Years Married to Wife
Respondent #1	52
Respondent #2	50
Respondent #3	20
Respondent #4	17
Respondent #5	45
Respondent #6	39
Respondent #7	12
Respondent #8	31
Respondent #9	34
Respondent #10	47

Table 4.7 Percentage of Respondents Previously Married

Previously Married	One Marriage
20%	80%
2 Respondents	8 Respondents

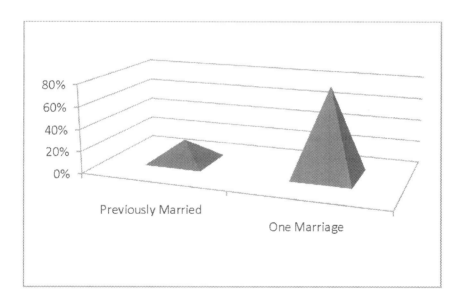

Table 4.8 Husbands with School-Aged Children

School-Aged Children	No School-Aged Children
20%	80%
2 Respondents	8 Respondents

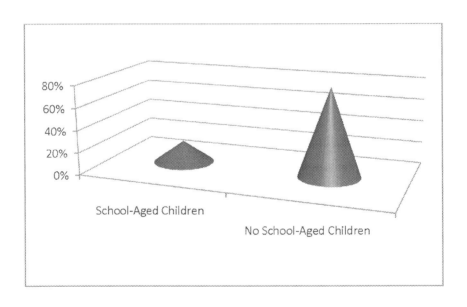

Table 4.9 Occupations of Husbands

Respondents	Occupations
Respondent # 1	Retiree/Full-Time Minister
Respondent #2	Educator
Respondent # 3	Church Musician
Respondent #4	Professional Bus/Truck Driver
Respondent # 5	Retired from Law Enforcement
Respondent #6	Security and Waiter
Respondent # 7	Maintenance Manager
Respondent #8	Retired Military/Part-Time Work
Respondent # 9	Minister and Educator
Respondent #10	Retired/Church Worker

Table 4.10 Comparison of Male and Female Leadership Traits of Pastors

Wife Of	Number of Male Characteristics	Number of Female Characteristics
Respondent #1	6	4
Respondent #2	6	5
Respondent #3	7	4
Respondent #4	No Response	No Response
Respondent #5	7	6
Respondent #6	No Response	No Response
Respondent #7	No Response	No Response
Respondent #8	No Response	No Response
Respondent #9	No Response	No Response
Respondent #10	5	6

General Elder Dr. Jacqueline Tuggle Taylor, Pastor and Deacon Jarris L. Taylor, Sr., First Gentleman

Our Ministry Journey 1978-Present

Reverend Taylor accepts her call into the ministry (1978, initial sermon preached at St. Paul Community Baptist Church)

Pastor Taylor and First Gentleman begins Pastoral Appointment in Baltimore, Maryland (1980, HOGC)

First Gentleman and Pastor Taylor assume Pastoral appointment in Harrisburg, Pennsylvania (1980s-1990s, HOGC)

Dr. Taylor and First Gentleman receives Pastoral Appointments in Baltimore City, Maryland (1990s) and Essex, Maryland (2011 – Present HOGC))

ABOUT THE AUTHOR

General Elder Dr. Jacqueline Taylor is the wife of Deacon Jarris Taylor, Sr., for forty-six years and the proud mother of four and grandmother of ten.

Her educational background includes a BA in theology from Virginia Theological Seminary, a MA in leadership in teaching and an Administrator I Certification from The College of Notre Dame of Maryland, a MDiv from the Eastern Baptist Theological Seminary of Lynchburg, Virginia, and a DMin in practical theology at Wesley Theological Seminary.

She served as an adjunct instructor teaching multiculturalism at the Johns Hopkins School of Medicine in collaboration with Clergy United for the Renewal of East Baltimore (Dr. Melvin B. Tuggle, II, CURE President) and Johns Hopkins Health Promotion (Dr. Diane Becker, Director). She also was the founder and organizer of the East Baltimore Reading and Resource Tutorial Program.

Her ministry work includes setting up churches and organizing Bible study groups in Baltimore City, Maryland, Altoona and Reading, Pennsylvania; she has served as pastor in Baltimore City and Essex, Maryland, and Harrisburg, Pennsylvania; conducted revival meetings in Maryland, Pennsylvania, Delaware, Tennessee, Washington DC, South Carolina, North Carolina, and New York.

General Elder work began in the State of Indiana in 2006. Presently, she is General Elder of Philadelphia, PA, Wilmington, DE, Alexandria and New Port News, Virginia. General Elder Taylor is also the "Servant Leader" (Pastor) of the House of God Church, Essex, Maryland.